LEXINGTON
in Good Taste

A Restaurant Guide
with Menus and Recipes

by Lani Basberg
and Jeanne Jennings

McClanahan
Publishing House

Library of Congress Catalog Card Number: 88 90 060663
International Standard Book Number: 0 913383 15 5

The menus shown are reproductions of the menus used in the restaurants. Some have been edited due to space limitations. Since the proprietors of the restaurants reserve the right to make changes in the content and prices contained on the menus, the publisher cannot be held responsible for any changes which are made after book publication.

Book and cover design by James Asher Graphics
Manufactured in the United States of America

All book correspondence should be addressed to:
McClanahan Publishing House, Incorporated
P.O. Box 100
Kuttawa, Kentucky 42055
(502) 388-9388
1-800-544-6959

INTRODUCTION

Lexington always brings to mind neatly manicured rolling hills of bluegrass, fragrant dogwood blossoms in the spring, football games in the fall, avid basketball fans, sleek thoroughbred horses, race tracks and a gentle, more relaxed way of life.

This is a city, however, that is vibrantly alive. Lexington enjoys its growing reputation as a place where you can see not only some of the best sports in the country, but enjoy outstanding cultural events from concerts to theater.

Here, in the center of what we call "God's Country", you can also sample some of the tastiest cuisine anywhere. From southern soul food to Indian, Chinese, Italian, Mexican, French or Continental, and from cafés to elegant dining rooms, Lexington has it all.

Lexington in Good Taste enables the reader to become aware of the wonderful wealth of restaurants in the Lexington area, their hours, location and menus. A general description is included to help you become more familiar with each restaurant. Also, through the generosity of the chefs, you may sample some of their best recipes in your own home.

People in Lexington believe they really have the best of everything. They must be right, as visitors each year include everyone from Hollywood actors to British royalty. Lexington is definitely a sophisticated and shining star in the bluegrass, and one that is always—in good taste.

DEDICATION

To
our wonderful parents:

Joseph and Imogene Coulter

Jim and Reaka Daniel

with
our love, respect and gratitude.

Lexington Fayette Urban County Government

SCOTTY BAESLER, Mayor

Stop! Take a few minutes to browse through this wonderful book which gives you a taste of Lexington. The sample menus and recipes will whet your appetite for an excellent lunch or dinner as well as the Bluegrass Area of Kentucky.

Lexington is a growing, dynamic city with many advantages of a major metropolis; but a 10-minute drive will have you in what one admirer called "America's only private national park." Enveloped within lush green acres bordered by miles of white plank fences, Lexington will welcome you warmly.

Relish the flavor of the Bluegrass found on these pages...but let it be only your first step. Come to Lexington for the real thing.

Sincerely,

Scotty Baesler
Mayor

LEXINGTON *in Good Taste*

TABLE OF CONTENTS

a la lucie

The eclectic style of the decor and the food at a la lucie create an atmosphere and a flair unequaled anywhere in Lexington. Chef and Proprietor Lucie Slone opened her restaurant on Halloween night 1985 and began serving "treats" that were and have continued to be hugely popular.

This is more than just another pretty restaurant. The tin ceiling, terrazzo floor, and deep, hot wall colors set off a truly unique collection of art and leafy green plants. The room reminds many of a restaurant in New York or Paris. Above all, it is comfortable and a perfect setting for good food and conversations.

A la lucie may be most famous for the variety of fresh seafood that is creatively prepared and served every night. Lucie prefers not to list seafood entrées on the menu in order to offer only those seasonally available. In addition to seafood, however, Lucie has white veal, beef, pork, and chicken on her regular menu, and a lengthy array of fresh vegetables. Desserts change nightly and will be described in luscious detail by your server.

At dinner each night, you can see Lucie's sister, Anne, serving as hostess, and Lucie, herself, busily checking on every aspect of the restaurant. Every so often Lucie kicks back, has a glass of wine, and enjoys her full house of guests. The superior staff seldom relaxes for a second, though, because Lucie says, "When visiting a la lucie, people expect a first rate dinner accompanied by excellent service". Since a la lucie is so much more, they also have a truly delightful evening!

Owner: Lucie Wellinghurst Slone
Address: 159 North Limestone
           Lexington, Kentucky 40507
Telephone: (606) 252-5277
Hours & Days: Monday-Saturday 6:00 pm until customers
           stop coming
           Closed all major holidays, the first week in
           January, and the first week in August
Reservations recommended
Visa, MasterCard, American Express, Diner's Club, Carte Blanche
Directions: Two blocks from Main Street on North Limestone
           on the left side of the street.

a la lucie

soups

Du Jour - Priced Daily   French Onion en Croute - $2.95

appetizers

Escargot in Mushroom Caps with Gruyere Cheese - $5.95
Escargot with Brie - $5.75
Escargot wrapped in Chicken with Garlic Butter - $7.50
Herring in White Wine $3.50
Smoked Salmon with Cream Cheese & Caviar - $6.50
Shrimp Steamed in Beer - $6.95
Goat Cheese in Pastry with Fruit - $6.95

Steak Tartar - $6.95   Artichoke Souffle $5.95

salads

Shrimp, Grapefruit & Avocado - $4.25   House Salad - $2.95
♥ ♥ ♥ Hearts of Romaine, Palm & Artichoke $3.95 ♥ ♥ ♥
Spinach Salad with Mandarin Oranges & Citrus Vinaigrette - $4.25
Caesar Nouvelle $4.50

a la lucie

entrees

New York Strip with Bearnaise $12.50

Tournedos aux Poivre or Naturel with
Bearnaise or Bordalaise $14.50

German-style Tenderloin $12.95
(Pickles, Dijon Mustard, Braised)

Filet Mignon with Bourbon Sauce $14.95

12 oz. T-Bone with Grilled Onions $12.95

Chicken Breast in Filo Dough with Hollandaise $11.50

Chicken with Tarragon & White Wine $11.50

Chicken Davida - $11.95
(Stuffed with Brie Cheese & Garlic with Tomato Sauce)

Veal aux Champignons - $14.95

Escalopes of Veal a la Viennoise $14.95

Sauteed Veal Marsale $14.95

Oriental Barbecue Pork Tenderloin - $12.95

Vegetable Plate $8.95

All entrees served with Salad & Vegetables.
Our server will describe the Seafood & Dessert selections.

159 North Limestone
Lexington, Ky. 40508
(606) 252-5277

Artichoke Hearts Stuffed with Goat Cheese

12 large artichoke hearts, canned
5 ounces goat cheese
Flour
Egg wash

Bread crumbs
Melted butter
Cocktail sauce

Open artichoke hearts in center and place 1 teaspoon goat cheese inside. Dredge hearts in flour, dip in egg wash, and roll in fresh bread crumbs. Place in pan and pour melted butter over top. Bake 10 minutes at 375 degrees or until bread crumbs are brown. Serve hot with cocktail sauce. Serves 4.

Chicken Wrapped in Filo

4 8-ounce chicken breasts,
   skinned
Poultry seasoning
White pepper
16 mushrooms
2 shallots

1 cup white wine
8 ounces Swiss cheese
8 sheets filo dough
1 pound unsalted butter
Hollandaise Sauce*

Sprinkle chicken breasts lightly with poultry seasoning and white pepper. Bake at 375 degrees for 10 to 15 minutes. Set aside to cool.

Chop mushrooms and shallots in food processor. Place in sauté pan, cover with wine, and cook until all liquid has evaporated. Set aside to cool. Cut cheese into 2-ounce chunks. Brush 2 sheets of filo dough with butter. Place chicken at one end and top with 2 tablespoons mushroom-shallot mixture and 2 ounces cheese. Fold in triangles (like you would fold the American flag), brush with butter, and bake at 375 degrees until golden brown. Serve with Hollandaise Sauce* or a cream sauce. Serves 4.

*See index

Conch Civiche

4 to 6 pieces conch meat
1 large red onion, chopped
1 large green or red pepper,
   chopped

2 to 4 jalapeño peppers,
   diced, to taste
3 to 4 limes

Flatten conch with hand. Add onions and peppers to conch. (Use more or less peppers according to individual taste.) Place limes in microwave about 1 minute. This helps to extract all juices. Squeeze juice over conch. Serve with saltine crackers.
Serves 4.

Grilled Marinated Swordfish

3 tablespoons soy sauce
3 tablespoons fresh orange juice
1 1/2 tablespoons olive oil
1 tablespoon tomato paste
1 tablespoon fresh parsley,
   chopped

2 garlic cloves, minced
1 tablespoon fresh lemon juice
1/4 teaspoon dried basil
1/4 teaspoon ground pepper
4 swordfish steaks,
   6 to 8 ounces each

Combine all ingredients except swordfish; mix well. Marinate swordfish, covered, for 1 hour, turning fish only once. Broil or grill swordfish 4 to 5 minutes each side. Serves 4.

Salmon with Cream Cheese Smoked Salmon Sauce

4 7-ounce fresh salmon or
   halibut filets
1 cup whipping cream
2 stalks green onions, chopped

4 ounces cream cheese
1 ounce smoked salmon,
   chunked

Grill, broil, or bake salmon.

While salmon is cooking, heat cream until bubbly. Add green onion and cream cheese. Whisk together until smooth. Stir in salmon chunks; pour sauce over cooked salmon filets. Serves 4.

Skate with Brown Butter

2 1/2 pounds skate wings
   (Rayfish), cleaned,
   cut into serving pieces
1/3 cup butter

1 tablespoon parsley, chopped
1 tablespoon capers, well drained
1 tablespoon lemon juice
Pinch cayenne pepper

Place skate in baking dish and bake at 375 degrees for 10 minutes. In sauté pan, heat butter until it foams and begins to brown. Blend in remaining ingredients; pour hot over fish. Serves 4.

Soft Shell Crab Stuffed with Crab Meat

6 or 7 fresh soft shell crabs
2 stalks celery, diced
1 large green or red pepper
1 bunch green onions, chopped
2 tablespoons Dijon mustard
8 ounces lump crabmeat
2 eggs
White pepper

1 tablespoon lemon juice
Flour
Egg wash
Bread crumbs
Melted butter
Remoulade Sauce* or
   cocktail sauce

Clean crabs. Cut face and pull top of crab away from bottom, leaving end attached.

Sauté celery, pepper, and onions until translucent, but still crunchy. Add mustard, crab, eggs, white pepper, and lemon; mix well. Place a large spoonful of mixture in each crab. Dredge crabs in flour, dip in egg wash, roll in bread crumbs, and coat with melted butter. Bake until brown. Serve with Remoulade Sauce or Cocktail Sauce. Serves 4 to 6.

*Remoulade Sauce
1 cup mayonnaise
1 tablespoon finely
  chopped pickle,
1 tablespoon capers,
  finely chopped
2 teaspoons prepared mustard

1 teaspoon parsley,
  finely chopped
1/2 teaspoon fresh tarragon,
  finely chopped
1/2 teaspoon chervil

Combine and refrigerate. Makes approximately 1 1/3 cups.

Dessert

Chocolate Ganache Torte

Pecan layer:

4 cups pecans, finely chopped
1 cup sugar

1/2 tablespoon salt
1 1/2 sticks butter, melted

Chocolate layer:

2 cups whipping cream
1 pound semi-sweet chocolate,
  small squares

1 stick butter
4 tablespoons light corn syrup

Coffee layer:

1 pound butter,
  room temperature
3 cups light brown sugar
4 ounces unsweetened chocolate,
  melted

7 large eggs
2 tablespoons instant coffee,
  more or less, to taste
Enough water to
  make coffee liquid

Garnish:

Coffee flavored whipped cream   Sugar flavored whipped cream

For pecan layer: Combine all ingredients, mixing well. Divide into 2 parts and press each part into a springform pan. Bake at 375 degrees until brown around the edges, about 10 minutes. Refrigerate when cooled.

For chocolate layer: Boil cream for 2 to 3 minutes. Remove from heat and add chocolate. When chocolate has melted, add butter and corn syrup, stirring well. Place pan in bowl of ice cold water and stir until chocolate is firm enough to spread onto pecan layers. Refrigerate again.

For coffee layer: Cream together butter and sugar. Stir in chocolate. Add eggs, two at a time, beating after each addition. Continue beating for approximately 10 minutes, or until mixture is no longer grainy. Add coffee. Do not overbeat or mixture will separate. If this happens, chill, and beat again. Place on top of other layers and refrigerate.

To serve, top with flavored whipped cream. Cut with hot knife. Makes 2 9 or 10-inch tortes. Serves 16.

A.P. Suggins Bar & Grill

A.P. Suggins Bar & Grill is that very special kind of eatery where old friends meet, new friends are made, and everyone is served a delicious home-cooked meal.

Suggins' menu alone should bring a smile to your face. It's actually seven full pages of wonderful foods, from appetizers to desserts. If beef, chicken, fish, Kentucky favorites, specialty burgers, salads with homemade soups, or Mexican food aren't enough, then check the long blackboard listing of today's specials and sniff the aroma of homemade rolls freshly baking in the kitchen. Now you can understand why some people eat here each and every day!

Suggins is strictly casual, with booths along the side, an assortment of chairs and tables in the middle, and snapshots of regular customers, family, and local celebrities lining the walls. One Lexington native who recently returned from several years out of state was heard remarking that he loves going to A.P. Suggins because "I always see people I know... some I haven't seen since childhood."

The man responsible for all this is Don Wathen, who opened Suggins in 1984. He grew up in the Chevy Chase area and rightly felt that a neighborhood restaurant would be enthusiastically supported. His father owned the successful Stirrup Cup Restaurant for forty years.

Apparently the same perfect ingredients for success are at work at A.P. Suggins today - if satisfied customers are any judge. People love the informal atmosphere, friendly service, and reasonable prices, but it's the inspired cooking, unadulterated by food trends, that keep them coming back.

Owner: Don Wathen
Address: 345 Romany Road
Lexington, Kentucky 40502
Telephone: (606) 268-0709
Hours & Days: Monday-Saturday 11:00 am to 11:00 pm
Closed Sundays
Visa, MasterCard, American Express
Directions: From Tates Creek Road, turn east onto Cooper Drive, then left onto Romany Road.

From Richmond Road, turn onto Chinoe, right onto Cochran, and left onto Romany.

Appetizers, Snacks and Lite Meals

Homemade Soup of the Day
Bowl $1⁹⁵
Cup $1⁷⁵

Buffalo-Style Chicken Wings
12 Zesty wings served in the
traditional buffalo way with
celery sticks & bleu cheese
dressing on the side $3⁹⁵

Fried Cheese - breaded to
order, served with a cup
of our famous chili for
for dipping $3⁹⁵

Double Order, 24 Wings, with
lots of celery & bleu cheese . $6⁹⁵

Golden Fried
Banana Peppers $2⁹⁵

Combo Platter - 3 banana
peppers, 3 potato skins &
½ order of mushrooms
with sauces for dipping
(no substitutes please) $4⁹⁵

Fresh Large Whole Mushrooms,
Fried Golden $2⁹⁵

Mexican Nachos - tortilla chips,
chili, cheddar cheese,
jalapenos, guacamole and
sour cream on request $4²⁵

Suggins Award Winning Chili -
with plenty of saltines
on the side $2⁵⁰
Cup of Chili $1⁹⁵

Suggins Chili - with cheddar
cheese, chopped onions, plus
tortilla chips for dipping $2⁹⁵

Suggins Beer Cheese Plate
with celery, radishes,
cracker basket $2⁹⁵

Suggins Chips & Don's
Homemade Salsa $1⁹⁵

POTATO SKINS
The Original
loaded with cheddar cheese
and bacon, sour cream
on the side $3⁹⁵

VEGGIE SKINS
Mushrooms, onions, & green
peppers, topped with
cheddar & parmesan cheese
& sour cream $4⁵⁰

Mexican Potato Skins
with chili, cheddar cheese,
guacamole, sour cream
and picante sauce $4⁵⁰

Golden Fried Onion Rings $2⁵⁰

Baked Potato with butter, sour
cream, cheddar cheese and
bacon $2⁷⁵

Salad

Our homemade salad dressings are ranch, blue cheese, honey-mustard, thousand island, french, garlic & olive oil vinegarette

House Salad - assorted greens
topped with bacon bits,
croutons, your choice of
homemade dressing $1⁹⁵

Taco Salad - chili, onions,
tomato, cheddar cheese, on
a bed of lettuce and served
in a flour tortilla shell with
picante sauce: Guacamole
and sour cream on request. $4⁵⁰

Southwest Chicken Salad -
chunks of spicy charbroiled
chicken served atop mixed
greens with black beans,
green onions, black olives,
cheddar cheese & finished
with our own homemade
salsa $4⁷⁵

Mediterranean Pasta Tuna Salad
w/feta cheese & black olives . $4⁵⁰

Chicken Salad Plate - fresh
chicken breast, mixed with
mayonnaise, celery, pecans,
a touch of seasoning,
surrounded with fresh fruit
& served with one of our
homemade muffins $4⁵⁰

Chef Salad - turkey, ham, swiss
and american cheese on a
bed of our tossed salad. With
sliced egg and our
homemade dressing $4⁷⁵

Cottage Cheese and fruit plate
with muffin $3⁵⁰

South of the Border

Chimichanga - Suggins chicken or beef chimichanga served on a bed
of lettuce with our homemade salsa and spicy black beans on the
side $4⁹⁵

Quesadilla - Chicken or beef on a flour tortilla with green peppers,
mushrooms and onions, served with homemade salsa and spicy black
beans $4⁷⁵

Mexican Pizza - A 12" pizza, enough for a crowd topped with our
famous chili, two kinds of cheeses, green pepper, black olives, onions
and mushrooms $4⁹⁵

Sandwiches

Vegetables or chips may be substituted for fries.

French Dip - hot choice roast beef sliced thinly & piled high on a hoagie roll with fries and au jus for dipping..... $4²⁵ with mozzarella or any cheese and grilled onions............add $.40

Catfish Sandwich - fried ocean catfish on a grilled buttered bun, served with fries...... $3⁹⁵

Grilled Chicken Club Sandwich - grilled chicken breast, and bacon, lettuce and tomato and swiss cheese on your choice of bun. Served with fries................... $4⁹⁵

Tuna Melt - tuna salad on an English muffin with swiss cheese, served with fries... $4²⁵

Rueben - grilled corned beef, sauerkraut and thousand island dressing on dark rye with fries.............. $3⁹⁵

Turkey, Swiss and Thousand Island Grill - fresh turkey, swiss cheese, thousand island dressing, grilled on wheat bread with fries.......... $3⁹⁵

Club Sandwich - a triple decker on your choice of bread with fries................... $4²⁵

Children's Corner

Plain Burger
served with fries........ $3⁵⁰

Grilled American Cheese Sandwich with fries....... $2⁸⁵

"PB & J" - peanut butter and jelly sandwich served with potato chips............. $1⁹⁵

Chili Cheese Dog with fries... $2⁸⁵

Plain Hot Dog with fries...... $2⁷⁵

Chicken Nuggets (6) served with french fries and sweet and sour sauce to dip with.. $2⁷⁵

All childrens items finished with Suggins homemade oatmeal raisin cookie.

Beef

10 oz. N.Y. Strip Steak - cut daily from our U.S. Choice strip loins - char-broiled to your taste, with two vegetables & house salad... $9²⁵

Suggins Special Bacon-wrapped Filet Mignon - a 7 oz. tenderloin served with two vegetables & house salad...........Market Price

Chopped Sirloin - ½ pound of choice chopped sirloin, broiled & topped with sauteed mushrooms, served with two vegetables & house salad................. $5⁹⁵

Open Faced Hot Roast Beef Sandwich - with brown gravy, mashed potatoes and your choice of one of our vegetables.............. $4⁹⁵

Suggins Tavern Beef - hardy portion of choice roast beef served au jus over pumpernickle with horseradish, with your choice of vegetable....... $4⁹⁵

Special Kentucky Favorites

Lamb Fries - golden fried lamb fries with our special cream sauce, choice of vegetable and potato and tossed salad................. $6⁹⁵

Fried Chicken Livers - served with special cream sauce and vegetable potato and tossed salad................. $6²⁵

Cold Plate - Baked country ham served on a platter, accompanied by warm roll, your choice of vegetable of the day and cole slaw...... $5⁵⁰

Vegetable Plate - choose any four of our side dishes (pick from vegetables of the day, cole slaw, cottage cheese, baked potato, mixed fresh fruit, served with warm roll. $4²⁵ any 3 with house salad..... $4⁷⁵

Fish and Chicken

Broiled Rainbow Trout, served with your choice of two vegetables and house salad. $7⁹⁵

Fried Catfish Dinner - Delta-raised catfish in corn meal, served with fries and homemade coleslaw....... $6²⁵ Also available broiled...... $6²⁵

Suggins Special Marinated Chicken - an 8 oz. boneless chicken breast, marinated in a light dressing to be extra moist, served with choice of two vegetables and tossed salad.................. $6²⁵

BBQ Chicken Dinner - 8 oz. charbroiled chicken breast, served with two vegetables & house salad........... $6²⁵

BBQ Chicken Club Dinner - 8 oz. charbroiled chicken breast, with cheddar cheese & two strips of crispy bacon, served with two vegetables & house salad........... $6⁷⁵

SUGGINS ORIGINAL HOT BROWN
Turkey and Country Ham on toast with our special cheese sauce, topped with tomato and bacon, served with tossed salad.................. $6⁷⁵

Ky. Style BBQ Sandwich - served on grilled bun with fries and homemade coleslaw............... $4⁵⁰

Burgers

100% choice beef ground daily for us. All burgers are served on a grilled buttered bun with lettuce, tomato, onion, pickle and fries. You may substitute vegetable of the day or cole slaw for fries. To substitute onion rings please add $.50.
Whole wheat bun available on request.

Vegetable

Baked Broccoli with Bleu Cheese Sauce

1 1/2 pounds broccoli
1/4 cup onion, chopped
2 tablespoons butter or
    margarine
2 tablespoons flour
1/4 teaspoon garlic salt

1 3-ounce package cream cheese
1/4 cup bleu cheese
1 2-ounce jar pimientos, sliced
1 cup milk
1/3 cup Ritz™ or butter crackers,
    crushed

Cook and drain broccoli; place in a greased, shallow baking dish. Set aside.

Cook onion in butter until soft. Stir in flour and garlic salt, cooking until bubbly. Remove pan from heat; mix in cream cheese, bleu cheese and pimientos. Gradually add milk, return to heat, and cook until sauce is thickened. Pour over broccoli, top with cracker crumbs, and bake at 350 degrees for 20 to 25 minutes. Serves 4.

Vegetable

Tomato-Spinach Casserole

1 10-ounce package
    frozen chopped spinach
1 tablespoon lemon juice
2 tablespoons sour cream
1/2 pound fresh mushrooms
2 tablespoons butter or
    margarine

2 tomatoes, sliced
1/2 teaspoon salt
1/2 teaspoon pepper
1/2 cup Parmesan cheese
1/2 cup Monterey Jack cheese,
    shredded

Cook and drain spinach; spread in bottom of a well-greased casserole. Sprinkle with lemon juice and dot with sour cream. Sauté mushrooms in butter for 2 minutes and pour over spinach. Top with tomatoes, and sprinkle with salt, pepper, and cheeses. Bake at 375 degrees until bubbly and hot, about 15 to 20 minutes. Serves 4.

Entrée

Eggplant and Tomato Tart

1 9-inch pastry shell, unbaked
1 small eggplant, about 1 pound
2 tablespoons olive oil
1 teaspoon dried basil leaves
1/2 teaspoon rosemary
2 tomatoes, peeled and sliced

1/4 teaspoon pepper
3 eggs, beaten
1 cup half & half
1/2 teaspoon salt
2/3 cup Parmesan cheese, grated

Bake pastry shell at 400 degrees for 15 minutes while preparing filling.

Cut eggplant into 1/4 inch slices. Cut slices into halves. Sauté in oil in frying pan for 5 minutes. Place on paper towels to drain. Sprinkle with basil and rosemary. Arrange eggplant and tomato slices in pastry shell. Sprinkle with pepper. Beat eggs with cream, salt, and 1/2 cup Parmesan cheese. Pour over eggplant and tomatoes, and sprinkle with remaining Parmesan cheese. Bake at 400 degrees for 10 minutes. Reduce heat to 350 degrees and bake for 30 minutes, or until center is set. Serve hot, warm, or at room temperature. This can be made ahead, refrigerated, and re-heated. Serves 4 to 6.

Flank Steak

Entrée

1 quart pineapple juice
1 pint soy sauce
1/8 cup brown sugar
1/8 cup sherry

1 cinnamon stick
2 1/2 pounds flank steak
Peppercorn Brown Sauce*

Mix pineapple juice, soy sauce, sugar, sherry, and cinnamon stick. Marinate steak in sauce for 12 hours. Bake marinated steak at 400 degrees for 20 to 25 minutes. Remove from pan, cut into strips across the grain, place on plate, and serve. Top with Peppercorn Brown Sauce. Serves 8.

*Peppercorn Brown Sauce:
1/2 stick butter
1 cup flour

4 beef bouillon cubes
4 cups water
1/4 cup fresh peppercorns

Make a roux with the butter and flour. Dissolve bouillon cubes in water; gradually add to roux, stirring until thickened. Add peppercorns. Serve over flank steak.

Chicken Croquettes

Entrée

2 1/2 pounds chicken, cooked
1 1/2 onions, finely diced
1/2 stalk celery, finely diced
1 1/2 teaspoons salt
1 1/2 teaspoons pepper

4 teaspoons oregano
6 eggs
1/2 box breading mix
Vegetable oil for deep frying
Lemon Sauce*

Mince chicken and add onions, celery, and spices. Mix well and add eggs. Mix well again and shape mixture into egg shaped croquettes. Roll in breading mix until thoroughly coated. Deep fry in oil until golden brown. Drain and serve with Lemon Sauce*. Serves 12.

*Lemon Sauce:
1 cup butter
1 cup flour

2 tablespoons chicken bouillon
1 quart water
1 tablespoon lemon pepper

Melt butter and add flour. Add chicken bouillon, mixed with water, and stir to make a roux. Cook until thickened and add lemon pepper. Serve over Chicken Croquettes.

Chocolate Pound Cake

1/2 cup butter, room temperature
1 1/2 cups sugar
4 1-ounce squares
  unsweetened chocolate, melted
4 eggs
2 1/2 cups flour

1/2 teaspoon baking soda
1 cup buttermilk
2 teaspoons vanilla
Quick Chocolate Frosting*
Walnut halves for garnish

Cream butter and sugar until well blended. Add chocolate and eggs; beat until smooth and fluffy. Add flour, baking soda, and buttermilk. Mix, using low speed, until blended. Stir in vanilla. Bake in a well-greased and floured 10-inch tube pan at 350 degrees for 45 to 55 minutes or until cake tester comes out clean. Cool 5 minutes, then remove from pan onto a wire rack. Cool completely. Spread with Quick Chocolate Frosting and garnish with walnut halves. Makes 1 10-inch tube cake.

*Quick Chocolate Frosting:
1 ounce unsweetened chocolate
1 tablespoon butter

1 cup unsifted powdered sugar
1 to 2 tablespoons hot coffee

Melt chocolate and butter in double boiler over hot water. Stir in sugar and just enough hot coffee to make a smooth, spreadable frosting.

Acajou

Lexington has a French-owned, French-managed, four star French restaurant and it's très magnifique! The owners, Alain Rochelmagne, and wife Eve, combined their considerable experience and creativity to open Acajou in 1987. Since then, it has been hailed by critics and patrons alike as the pièce de résistance in fine gourmet dining.

Acajou is located in a restored 19th century building with great, shiny, mahogany double doors (Acajou is French for mahogany). High ceilings, paddle fans, floral bordered pale peach walls, and Toulouse Lautrec prints set the atmosphere to the turn of the century in Paris, France. On Friday and Saturday evenings you'll hear melodies by Gershwin, Porter, and others being played by Mike Allen on the baby grand piano. A classic mahogany bar frames one side of the dining room where guests are delighted with such international favorites as peach champagne, negroni, and salzarac.

Once seated, tuxedoed waiters immediately appear to serve. While choosing from an impressive wine list, you are treated to complimentary "amuse bouchée" (canapés). Highlights from the menu include such delectables as Assiette de Trois Filets - loins of pork and of veal, each filet served in a different sauce, an ambitious mélange of color and flavor.

Acajou's own pastry chef prepares all the deliciously decadent desserts as well as the palate cleansing sorbets. Suffice it to say, you will agree with Louisville Courier Journal's restaurant critic, Robin Garr, when he reports, "Impeccable elegance rules at Acajou....I want to go back. Now."

Owners: Alain and Eve Rochelmagne
Address: 265 North Limestone
          Lexington, Kentucky 40507
Telephone: (606) 233-7778
Hours & Days: Monday-Thursday 6:00 pm to 10:00 pm
                 Friday-Saturday 6:00 pm to 10:30 pm
                 Sunday evenings only during horse sales or private parties
Reservations recommended
Visa, MasterCard, American Express
Directions: Downtown corner of North Limestone and Third Streets.
           Valet service available.

Acajou
FRENCH RESTAURANT

Soups

Le Potage D'hiver aux herbes fraiches........ 4⁷⁵
Winter vegetable cream soup

Velouté de homard parfumé au saffran....... 5⁵⁰
Lobster cream soup flavored with saffron

Appetizers

Felliðleté D'Escargots au beurre D'Arômates
champignons sauvages et jus de thym......... 7⁹⁵
Snails in puff pastry with a garlic and herb butter,
wild mushrooms and thyme sauce

Terrine de Saumon et Sᵗ Jacques, crème de persil
et caviar d'esturgeon................... 7⁵⁰
Terrine of salmon and scallops served with a
parsley sauce and sturgeon caviar

Mousse de tomates à L'Estragon et mousse
d'artichauds sur coulis de tomates rôties au
gingembre et crème de cresson............... 6²⁵
Tarragon flavored tomato mousse served with a
watercress sauce and artichoke mousse with roasted
tomato and ginger sauce

Salade au crotin de chauvignol à l'huile de trûffe
palm grillé à l'ail..................... 8²⁵
Warm goat cheese salad with a truffle oil vinaigrette
and garlic toast

Medaillon de Foie Gras au naturel........... 15²⁵
Medallion of Foie Gras

Caviar de Beluga et sa vodka.......... 45⁰⁰
Baluga caviar and vodka

Salade verte maison au vinaigre de framboise 3⁷⁵
Mixed green salad with raspberry vinaigrette

Winter Menu Selection

Main Courses

Suprème de canard au citrus et son flan à l'orange, ris sauvage aux zestes et lardons 18⁹⁵
Breast of duck and orange flan with a citrus sauce served with wild rice

Roulade de poulet farcie de sa mousse homardière sur galette de pomme de terre au thym 15⁹⁵
Breast of chicken stuffed with lobster mousse and served on a bed of sliced thyme flavored potatoes

Carré d'agneau rôtis aux herbes de provence et julienne des deux choux aux petits lardons 21⁹⁵
Roasted rack of lamb with herbs of provence and julienne of red and green cabbage

Côte de veau sautée aux poivres verts et pâtes fraiches à la crème de proscuitto 20⁹⁵
Sauted veal chop in green peppercorn sauce with fresh pasta and proscuitto ham sauce

Filet de boeuf aux échalottes rôtes jus de trûffe et symphonie de courgettes au thym 19⁹⁵
Tenderloin of beef and roasted shallots served with squash and truffle sauce

Homard de Maine farcie de sa mousse de crevettes julienne de légume et sauce vanille 21⁹⁵
Fresh Maine lobster stuffed with shrimp mousse, served on a bed of julienne vegetables and vanilla sauce

Tresse de saumon et sole de douvre dans un beurre de fleure de lavande et petits légumes tournés 20⁹⁵
Norwegian salmon and dover sole with lavander flower butter sauce and vegetables

*If a dish is missing today from our menu, do not be disappointed —
the quality required was not available from the market selection.*

At the request of our patrons, we ask that you please refrain from cigar smoking.

Thank You

— Acajou

Entrée

Beef Tenderloin with Green Pepper Sauce

2 pounds beef tenderloin
2 teaspoons butter
3 shallots or 1/2 onion,
  coarsely chopped
2 teaspoons green peppercorns
4 teaspoons brandy

4 cups beef stock
1 cup cream
4 teaspoons butter
4 teaspoons flour
Salt and pepper to taste

Cook beef tenderloin to desired doneness.

For sauce: Blend butter and shallots in pan over high heat and sauté until the color of hazelnuts. Add green peppercorns, brandy, and beef stock. Allow to boil for 15 minutes. Stir in cream and heat thoroughly. In another bowl, mix butter and flour to make a roux. Add roux to boiling sauce and whisk until smooth. Season to taste with salt and pepper. This sauce can also be served with white or dark meat. Serves 8.

Entrée

Boeuf Bourguignonne

5 to 6 pounds stew beef
Butter
Vegetable oil
4 large carrots,
  sliced 1/4 inch thick
5 onions, chopped in large pieces
4 to 5 cloves garlic
Salt and pepper to taste
Nutmeg

Whole cloves
Thyme
Chopped bay leaf
2 tablespoons flour
Red wine
5 to 6 cups beef stock
8 potatoes, peeled and steamed
Parsley
Macaroni, noodles, or rice

Sauté meat in butter and oil; add carrots, onions, garlic, salt, and pepper. Add spices, flour to thicken, lots of red wine and beef stock. Place mixture in large roaster and bake at 400 to 500 degrees for 1 to 2 hours. Peel and steam potatoes and add parsley. To serve, transfer stew to large casserole, place potatoes around edge and serve with macaroni, noodles, or rice. Serves 8.

Entrée

Chicken with Leeks

3 leeks
Cold water
6 to 9 tablespoons vinegar
Salt and pepper to taste

Oil and butter for sautéing
6 chicken breasts, whole,
  boned and skinned
6 to 9 tablespoons heavy cream

Soak leeks in cold water with vinegar. Split leeks, starting from bottom; clean and chop. Season with salt and pepper. Sauté in oil and butter until crisp.

Butter area where chicken will lie on foil. Place leeks on one side of chicken breasts. Fold other side over. Pour 2 to 3 tablespoons heavy cream over chicken. Wrap foil tightly and cook at 350 degrees for 25 minutes. With leftover leeks, add more cream, heat, and pour over chicken breasts. Serves 6.

Norwegian Salmon with White Butter Sauce

Entrée

2 pounds salmon filets
Salt and pepper
2 cups white wine

3 shallots or 1/2 onion, chopped
1 cup heavy cream
1 pound unsalted butter

Cut 8 portions of salmon. Place them in pan with salt and pepper and 1 cup white wine. Refrigerate while preparing White Butter Sauce.

For White Butter Sauce: Using a copper or stainless steel pan, combine 1 cup white wine and chopped shallots; reduce until just 3 tablespoons sauce remain. Add cream and reduce in half. Keep boiling while adding butter, a small amount at a time. Whisk strongly and adjust seasonings. This sauce may be used plain, or fresh herbs can be added.

Cook salmon in pre-heated 250 degree oven for 10 minutes. Place salmon on a plate and drizzle warm sauce over top. Serve with fresh pasta or rice. Serves 8.

Sea Scallops with Virgin Sauce

Entrée

1 bunch parsley
1 bunch chives
7 shallots or 1 onion
3 garlic buds
1 cup olive oil
2 tomatoes, diced

Juice of 3 lemons
3 pinches salt
2 pinches black pepper
Lettuce or salad greens
Oil for cooking
1 pound sea scallops

For Virgin Sauce: Chop parsley, chives, shallots, and garlic. Place in plastic container with olive oil. Add tomatoes, lemon juice, salt, and pepper. Set aside.

Wash lettuce or salad greens and place in middle of each plate. Heat oil in large skillet over high heat. When oil starts to steam, add sea scallops. Combine Virgin Sauce with scallops; simmer for several minutes. Sea scallops should remain soft. Pour over tops of salads. Serves 8.

Dessert

Anglaise Crème

8 egg yolks
1 1/4 cups sugar
1 vanilla bean, split
4 cups milk

Coffee powder, cocoa powder,
Grand Marnier,
    or coffee liqueur (optional)

Whisk eggs and sugar. Add vanilla bean to milk and bring to a boil. Add 1 optional ingredient, if desired. Add milk to eggs and sugar and heat to thicken. Strain hot liquid into mixing bowl. Place milk mixture (in bowl) on ice cubes inside a larger bowl to stop cooking quickly. Stir occasionally until cooled. Serves 8.

Dessert

Floating Island Meringues

8 egg whites, room temperature
8 tablespoons sugar
Pinch of cream of tartar

Melted butter
Sugar to coat ramekins

Whip egg whites until foamy. Add sugar and cream of tartar, whipping until stiff. Grease 6 ramekins with melted butter and coat with sugar. Fill with egg white mixture and place in pan of hot water. Bake at 400 degrees for 4 to 5 minutes. Unmold and refrigerate until ready to use. Serves 6.

Alfalfa

If you thought Alfalfa was a hippie, "nuts and twigs" health food restaurant serving only tofu and sprouts...boy, were you wrong! Alfalfa does proudly wear the "health-conscious" label, however, serving wholesome, organically grown foods and many vegetarian dishes. They place a great deal of importance on acquiring ingredients that will enhance the customer's health, as well as the environment. Yet, they are much, much more. They prepare meat dishes, a multitude of ethnic foods, updated local favorites, homemade rolls, and sinfully rich desserts.

The handwritten menu at Alfalfa changes every day and there are actually more specials listed on the chalk boards than the menus! The imaginative way Alfalfa prepares beef, chicken, fish, and vegetables boggles the mind and tantalizes the palate. Whoever thought up Country Ham and Apple Quiche, Curried Cabbage, Greek Zucchini Soup, and Cream Cheese Cherry Pie has my respect and my gratitude forever. Servings at Alfalfa are large and satisfying, and are accompanied by house salads and homemade bread. They make all of their own breads and desserts from scratch at Alfalfa and the freshness and taste cannot be beat!

The comfortable two-room dining area has not changed much through the years. It feels as warm and cozy as grandmother's kitchen. Alfalfa has been in operation for two decades, and its owners constantly strive to keep the same high quality, creative cuisine, reasonable prices, and casual, laid back atmosphere for which they are so famous.

Owners: Peter Fleming
              Jake Gibbs
              Jim Happ
              Cathy and Tom Martin
Address: 557 South Limestone
              Lexington, Kentucky 40508
Telephone: (606) 253-0014
Hours & Days: Lunch: Monday-Friday 11:00 am to 2:00 pm
                    Dinner: Tuesday-Thursday 5:30 pm to 9:00 pm
                            Friday-Saturday 5:30 pm to 10:00 pm
                    Brunch: Saturday-Sunday 10:00 am to 2:00 pm
Reservations not required
No credit cards. Checks are accepted.
Directions: South Limestone directly across the street from
              the University of Kentucky's School of Business
              and Economics.

ALFALFA

LUNCH
MON-FRI 11:00 - 2:00

Today's Soups
- tomato florentine
- vegetable beef

SALADS

House
small... 1.95
large... 3.25

CHEF... 4.25

SPROUT... 4.00

YOGURT & FRUIT... 2.75

SANDWICHES
on our homemade wholewheat bread
COUNTRY HAM ... 4.75
ALFALFA AVACADO GRILL... 4.25
GRILLED CHEESE & TOMATO... 2.75
TUNA SALAD... 2.75
EGG SALAD... 2.50
TOFU SPREAD ON PITA BREAD... 2.75
PEANUT BUTTER, BANANA, & RASIN ... 2.50
OLIVE NUT... 2.35

BRUNCH SPECIALS
served w/ wholewheat bread

HUEVOS RANCHEROS two poached eggs over rice w/ rancheros sauce - topped w/ green peppers, onion, & cheddar cheese. 3.95

AVACADO & CHEDDAR OMLETE a three egg omlete filled w/ avacado & cheddar cheese. 4.75

SPANISH OMLETE a three egg omlete filled w/ onions, green peppers, cheddar cheese. topped w/ rancheros sauce. 4.50

MATZO BREI fresh sautee'd onions, green peppers, mushrooms, pan-fried w/ eggs, matzo crackers. w/ sour cream. 3.75

TODAY'S SPECIAL'S

CHICKEN STROGANOFF... 4.55
GREEK SPINACH PIE ... 4.25
ROTINI PESTO ... 3.95
BROCCOLI-TOMATO RAREBIT... 3.95
BLACK BEANS & SALSA ... 3.95
SOUR CREAM BEAN BURRITOS... 3.95
EGGPLANT CREOLE ... 3.75
TOFU CHILI-FRIED RICE... 3.75
SWISS MUSHROOM QUICHE ... 3.95
VEGETARIAN CHILI ... 3.95
CHILI ... 2.95
RED BEANS & RICE ... 3.75
HOPPIN' JOHN ... 3.75

ALFALFA

all entrees are served w/ house salad & homemade bread.

SALMON GISERAND 10⁹⁵

Salmon fillets baked in white wine & served w/ a cream sauce flavored w/ tomatoes, garlic & lemon juice. Served w/ choice of brown rice, tonite's vegetable or spinach noodles.

CHICKEN SARDOU 9⁹⁵

Sauteéd chicken breasts on a bed of creamed spinach, topped w/ a rich hollandaise sauce & artichoke slices. Served w/ choice of brown rice, spinach noodles, or tonite's vegetable.

TROUT ALMONDINE 8⁹⁵

Fresh trout breaded in almond flour & panfried. Served w/ homemade tartar sauce & choice of spinach noodles, brown rice or tonite's vegetable.

CHICKEN TALESE 8⁹⁵

Sauteéd chicken breasts served on a bed of fresh spinach. Topped w/ fresh sauteéd mushrooms & a creamy swiss sauce. w/ choice of brown rice, tonite's vegetable, or spinach noodles.

BEEF BURRITOS 7⁵⁰

Flour tortillas stuffed w/ tender beef, refried beans, white cheddar cheese, sour cream & spices. Topped w/ a zesty huevos sauce. Served w/ brown rice.

VIETNAMESE CHICKEN STEW 7²⁵

A fiery chicken stew w/ onions, fresh basil, hot peppers, & rice vinegar. Served over brown rice or spinach noodles. Not for the faint of heart!

LASAGNA ALFALFA 6⁷⁵

Spinach, ricotta & mozzarella cheese layered between lasagna noodles. Topped w/ our own marinara sauce.

FETTUCINE ALFREDO 6⁷⁵

Fettucine pasta tossed w/ a delicious parmesan-garlic cream sauce.

QUICHE
almond apple & brie
SOUPS
lentil, chicken mushroom
VEGETABLE
broccoli w/ lemon butter

SWISS VEGETABLE CREPES 6²⁵

Our own crepes filled w/ sauteéd fresh vegetables. Topped w/ swiss sauce. Served w/ choice of brown rice, spinach noodles, or tonite's vegetable.

SESAME TOFU STEW 5⁷⁵

A non-dairy vegetable stew of onions, carrots mushrooms, green pepper, broccoli & tofu in a sauce of miso, tahini, garlic & ginger. Served over brown rice or spinach noodles.

HOPPIN JOHN 5⁵⁰

Black-eyed peas on a bed of brown rice. Topped w/ a zesty tomato sauce, white cheddar cheese, green pepper & onion.

Hummus
(Middle Eastern Dip or Spread)

3 cups garbanzo beans,
  home cooked or canned
2 tablespoons bean water
  from cooking or can
1/3 cup tahini*
1 tablespoon olive oil
Juice of 1 lemon

1 tablespoon red wine vinegar
1/4 cup scallions, finely chopped
1/4 cup parsley, finely chopped
2 cloves garlic, minced
Pinch cayenne pepper
Salt and pepper to taste

Using a food processor, blender, or potato masher, mash beans and bean water well. Add tahini, oil, lemon juice, and vinegar, and blend thoroughly. Add remaining ingredients and blend well. Makes approximately 3 cups.

* sesame butter, available in health food stores or in health food department of grocery stores

Gazpacho

46 ounces tomato juice
1 green pepper, chopped
1/2 cucumber, diced
3 fresh tomatoes, chopped
1/2 cup chopped parsley
1 small onion, chopped
1 clove garlic, minced
Juice of 1 lemon

2 tablespoons red wine vinegar
2 tablespoons olive oil, optional
1 teaspoon basil
Salt to taste
Pepper to taste
Worcestershire sauce to taste
Tabasco sauce to taste

Place all ingredients in a large bowl. Stir thoroughly to mix. Chill at least 2 hours before serving. The flavor is even better the next day. Serves 6 to 8.

Alfalfa House Salad

1/2 green cabbage, grated
1/2 red cabbage, grated
2 carrots, grated
1/2 rib celery, finely chopped
6 rings green pepper

6 cherry tomatoes
6 slices cucumber, unpeeled
6 small bunches alfalfa sprouts
6 teaspoons sunflower seeds

Place enough of first 4 ingredients in 6 salad bowls to almost fill them. Garnish with green peppers, tomatoes, cucumbers, and sprouts. Sprinkle sunflower seeds over the tops. Serve with Herb Dressing or dressing of your choice. Serves 6.

Herb Dressing

2/3 cup vegetable oil
1/3 cup red wine vinegar
1/2 teaspoon basil
1/2 teaspoon oregano

1/2 teaspoon dry mustard
Salt
Pepper

Place all ingredients in a glass jar and screw lid on tightly. Shake well to blend. Keeps well in refrigerator. Makes 1 cup.

Alfalfa Avocado Grill

2 slices firm whole wheat bread
4 tablespoons hummus
   (see recipe)
1 slice Swiss cheese

2 slices tomato
1 slice cheddar cheese
2 slices avocado

Spread 2 tablespoons hummus on each piece of bread. Place Swiss cheese and tomato on one half and cheddar cheese and avocado on other half. Place both halves of sandwich, bread side down, in a skillet covered with melted butter or margarine. Cook over low heat until both cheeses are melted. Assemble sandwich by carefully putting both halves together. Cut in half and serve immediately. Serves 1.

Chicken Talese

Sauce:
1 tablespoon butter
1 tablespoon flour
Pinch nutmeg
Salt and pepper to taste
1 cup milk
1/2 cup grated Swiss cheese
1 tablespoon Parmesan cheese,
   grated

Chicken:
2 eggs
4 chicken breasts,
   skinned and boned
1/2 cup flour
3 tablespoons oil
1/2 pound mushrooms
8 ounces spinach, washed,
   and torn into bite-size pieces

For sauce: Melt butter in saucepan, stir in flour. Cook over low heat until smooth, stirring constantly. Add seasonings. Continue stirring while slowly adding milk. Slowly add cheeses, continuing to stir until smooth. Cook until sauce begins to thicken, stirring occasionally.

For chicken: Beat eggs lightly. Dip each piece of chicken in egg and then in a light coating of flour. Sauté in oil until both sides are brown. Add mushrooms at the end of cooking and sauté until mushrooms are brown. Arrange chicken and mushrooms on a bed of spinach and top with sauce. Serves 4.

Entrée

Creole Cabbage

3 tablespoons vegetable oil
1 onion, chopped
1 clove garlic, minced
1/2 head of cabbage,
  cut into 1/2 inch slices
1 green pepper, chopped
2 ribs celery, chopped
3 cups tomatoes, diced

Juice of 1 lemon
1/2 teaspoon salt
1/8 teaspoon pepper
1 bay leaf
1 teaspoon oregano
Dash Worcestershire sauce
Dash Tabasco sauce
2 tablespoons brown sugar

Heat oil in a large skillet or soup pot; sauté onions and garlic until onions are transparent. Add cabbage, green pepper, and celery; continue to cook for 15 minutes or until cabbage is cooked, but still slightly crisp. Crush or mash tomatoes to break up any large pieces. Add to cabbage along with accompanying tomato juice. Add remaining ingredients, stirring well. Simmer until tender, approximately 30 minutes. Serves 6.

Entrée

Zucchini Cassalinga

1/2 cup Parmesan cheese
1/4 cup chopped pecans
1 tablespoon basil
1/4 teaspoon garlic powder
1/8 teaspoon black pepper

1 medium zucchini,
  unpeeled and chopped
1 onion, chopped
1 tablespoon olive oil
3 cups cooked fettucine

Combine cheese, pecans, basil, garlic powder, and pepper. Sauté zucchini and onions in oil approximately 2 minutes. Add cheese mixture and stir only until heated. Toss with cooked fettucine. Serves 4.

Dessert

Whole House Cookies

1 1/2 cups whole wheat
  pastry flour
1 tablespoon baking powder
1 tablespoon cinnamon
1/4 teaspoon ginger
1/2 teaspoon salt
1 1/4 cups rolled oats
1 1/2 cup raisins
1 cup walnuts, chopped

1 cup pecans, chopped
1 cup almonds, chopped
1/2 cup sunflower seeds, hulled
1/2 cup sesame seeds
1/2 pound butter, softened
1/2 cup natural peanut butter
2 eggs
1 cup honey

In a large bowl, sift together flour, baking powder, cinnamon, ginger, and salt. Stir in oats, raisins, nuts, and seeds. In a separate bowl, cream together butter, peanut butter, eggs, and honey. Mix wet and dry ingredients together. For each cookie, drop 1/4 cup of dough on a greased or no-stick baking sheet. Bake at 350 degrees for 18 minutes until lightly browned and semi-firm. Makes 2 dozen large cookies.

Amato's

Jim Amato opened this popular restaurant in 1986, and with it revived a rich family tradition of Italian cuisine that has flourished in Lexington for more than half a century. Amato, a former Mayor of Lexington, is a second generation restauranteur. His father, Matthew, owned and operated several restaurants in Lexington since the 1920's and began the culinary legacy.

Located in the historic and beautiful West Jefferson Place, Amato's occupies the West Wing of this former dormitory and nursing school. The original paneled walls and terrazzo floor of the main dining room were refurbished and the magnificent mahogany bar in another area came from a turn of the century Lexington landmark, "Pop" Gruner's Main Spring Saloon. In the "Mayor's Room", photos of Lexington's past and present leaders cover the wall, and an elaborate Italian marble fireplace from the early 19th century is highlighted.

Amato's menu showcases Northern Italian cuisine such as Venetian Grilled Chicken, Southern Italian dishes such as Lasagna and Veal Parmesan, fresh fish, chicken, beef, and plenty of pasta. If it all sounds so good that you cannot possibly decide, a Combo Meal of three choices will delight and satisfy. After dinner coffees with delicious names like Almond Amaretto, Dutch Chocolate, and Hazelnut compete with a mouth-watering array of desserts to complete your meal.

In a world of sparse style and shortcuts on quality, Amato's brings back pleasure, plentitude, and a genuine warmth that continually attracts a crowd.

Owner: Tracy W. Farmer
Address: 535 West Second Street
         Lexington, Kentucky 40508
Telephone: (606) 255-7954
Hours & Days: Lunch: Monday-Friday 11:30 am to 5:00 pm
              Dinner: Monday-Thursday 5:00 pm to 10:00 pm
              Friday-Saturday 5:00 pm to 11:00 pm
Reservations suggested
Visa, MasterCard, American Express, Discover, Diner's Club, Carte Blanche
Directions: Main Street to North Broadway; two lights and
            turn left onto Second Street; corner of Second
            and Jefferson Streets in the West Jefferson Place.

Appetizers

Provolone Marinara
Coated with seasoned bread crumbs, lightly fried, and topped with marinara.   **$3.75**

Manzo Mushrooms
Large fresh mushrooms stuffed with spicy sausage and peppers. Topped with parmesan cheese and baked.   **$3.95**

Amato Misto
Our favorite, a sampling of provolone marinara, toasted ravioli and manzo mushrooms.
Serves two.   **$5.95**

Calamari Fritti
Breaded and seasoned rings of toasted squid served with honey mustard sauce. **$3.95**

Toasted Ravioli
Pasta pockets stuffed with Italian cheese and meat, lightly fried, and served with marinara sauce for dipping.   **$3.45**

Fettuccine Alfredo
Our own pasta topped with creamy garlic cheese sauce.   **$2.95**

Mozzarella Dijon
Breaded mozzarella cheese layered with Italian ham and lightly fried, served with Dijon sauce.   **$3.95**

Pizza Salcicce
A 9" pizza, smothered with marinara sauce, green peppers, and spicy sausage. **$3.95**

Pizza Bianco
A 9" pizza, topped with mushrooms, onions, three cheeses, and a hint of pesto. **$3.95**

Extra Ingredients   45¢

Soups

Minstrone Amato
Classic Italian soup filled with sausage, vegetables, and pasta. **Bowl $2.95 Cup $1.95**

Baked Onion Soup
Savory sauteed onions in a rich beef broth topped with robust provolone cheese.
Bowl $3.45 Cup $2.25

Salad

Served with Amato's warm garlic bread.

Amato's Salad
Fresh iceberg lettuce, spinach, tomato, pepperoncinis, red onions, olives and fresh ingredients of the day from the green grocer. Tossed with Amato's House dressing.   **$3.95**

Pasta

All entrees served with unlimited house salad and garlic breadsticks.

Spaghetti		**Fettuccine**	
With our own sausage	**$6.95**	Alfredo	**$6.95**
With meat sauce	**$6.95**	Primavera (cream and vegetables)	**$7.95**
With marinara	**$5.95**	Chicken Primavera	**$8.95**
With meatballs	**$6.95**	Di Polla Pomodoro	
Linguini		(chicken and sundried tomatos)	**$9.25**
With red or white clam sauce	**$8.95**		
Carbonara (bacon and peas)	**$9.45**		
Di Pesce (shrimp and crab)	**$9.95**		

Manicotti
Pasta filled with a blend of three different cheeses. Baked and topped with marinara. **$7.50**

Canneloni
Italian sausage and beef filled crepes topped with cheese and marinara.   **$7.95**

Lasagna
Layers of mozzarella and provolone cheeses, hearty meat sauce and pasta. Baked to order.
$8.95

Egg Plant Parmesan
Tender slices of breaded egg plant baked with cheese and marinara.   **$7.50**

Combo Meals

Guisto Misto
Veal Marsala, Venetian Grilled Chicken and Fettuccine Alfredo. $11.45
Pasta Misto
Spaghetti with meat sauce, Manicotti, Canneloni and Italian sausage. $11.45
Northern
Veal Piccata, Venetian Grilled Chicken and Fettuccine Alfredo. $12.45
Southern
Lasagna, Chicken Parmesan and Fettuccine Alfredo. $11.95
Grilled Sausage
A platter of grilled Italian sausage, peppers and Fettuccine Alfredo. $9.95

Pasta Vivita (To Life)

Healthy pasta dishes low in cholesterol, sodium, and calories.

Mesquite Grilled Chicken
A boneless chicken breast charbroiled and seasoned with mesquite. Served with steamed vegetable of the day. $8.95
Halibut Kabobs with Linguini Aglio Olio
Two skewers of halibut chunks and garden vegetables served over linguini. $12.95
Pineapple Primavera Aceto
Linguini and garden vegetables sauteed in a light ginger pineapple juice vinaigrette. $6.95

Veal

Veal Parmesan
Center cut top round of veal lightly breaded and fried. Topped with marinara and mozzarella. $13.95
Veal Piccata
Lightly sauteed and finished with butter, white wine, capers, lemon and parsley. $13.95
Veal Zefferino
Lightly sauteed with mushrooms and walnuts in a rich demi-glaze and white wine sauce. $13.95
Veal Marsala
Sauteed with whole butter, Marsala wine, in a sauce of mushrooms, fresh tomatos, garlic and demi-glaze. $13.95

Chicken

Chicken Marco Polo
Boneless breast sauteed with shrimp, asparagus, cream and herbs. $11.45
Chicken Parmesan
Boneless breast rolled in seasoned cheese and bread crumbs, lightly fried and topped with marinara, mozzarella and parmesan cheeses. $9.45
Chicken Tetrazzini
A baked chicken casserole with spaghetti, sherry, cream and mushrooms, mozzarella and parmasan cheeses. $9.45
Chicken Piccata
Lightly sauteed and finished with butter, white wine, capers, lemon and parsley. $9.45
Chicken Marsala
Sauteed with whole butter, Marsala wine, in a sauce of mushrooms, fresh tomatos, garlic and demi-glaze. $9.65

From the Char-Broiler

Broiled Lamb Chops
Three lamb chops char-broiled to perfection and served with mint jelly. $16.95
Steak Bordolino
A 12 oz. New York strip char-broiled. Topped with sauteed mushrooms, scallions, and red wine. $15.95
Venetian Grilled Chicken
Marinated breast of chicken char-broiled and topped with olives and cheese. $9.95
Strip Steak Florentine
A 12 oz. strip brushed with olive oil and seasonings, char-broiled and topped with Delmonico onions. $14.95
Broiled Shrimp Scampi
Shrimp broiled in garlic herb butter, dusted with parmesan and bread crumbs. $11.95
Fresh Fish of the Day
Ask your server.   **Market Price**

Manzo Mushrooms

Stuffing Mix:
1/2 pound ground beef
1/2 pound Italian sausage
1 tablespoon garlic cloves,
  chopped

1/2 pound frozen,
  chopped spinach
3 tablespoons Parmesan cheese
1/4 tablespoon salt
1/4 tablespoon black pepper

Brown beef and sausage with garlic; drain. Add spinach, cheese, and spices. Mix thoroughly and set aside to cool.

Mushroom Caps:
50 medium-size mushroom caps
1/4 cup lemon juice in
  1 quart water

1 large green bell pepper, diced
1 large red bell pepper, diced
1 cup Parmesan cheese
1 stick butter, melted

Break stems from caps, clean, and wash in lemon water. Place in shallow baking dish and fill each cap with stuffing mixture. Sprinkle diced peppers on top. Pour melted butter over all the caps and sprinkle with Parmesan cheese. Bake in pre-heated 425-degree oven for 10 minutes. Makes 50 mushroom caps.

Minestrone Soup

1 pound bulk Italian sausage
1/2 gallon water
1 teaspoon chicken base
1/2 cup carrots, peeled and sliced
1 stalk celery, diced
1 cup onion, diced
1 cup zucchini, diced

1/2 cup red bell pepper, diced
1/2 cup green bell pepper, diced
1 cup sliced red cabbage
1 pint Marinara sauce
3 tablespoons rosemary
1/2 pound rotini pasta
3 ounces Parmesan cheese

Brown sausage and drain off excess grease. Add water and chicken base, and bring to a boil in a 1 gallon stock pot. Add remaining ingredients and bring to a boil. Reduce heat, and simmer for 1 hour. Portion into bowls and sprinkle with Parmesan cheese. Yields 3 quarts.

Tomato, Mozzarella, and Basil Salad

6 medium tomatoes,
  sliced 1/4-inch thick
1/2 pound fresh Mozzarella
  cheese, sliced

6 ounces olive oil
1 bunch fresh basil leaves
Salt and pepper to taste

Using 6 salad plates, alternate tomatoes (1 tomato per plate) with Mozzarella cheese. Pour 1 ounce olive oil over each plate, and sprinkle with chopped basil. Season to taste with salt and pepper, and garnish each with 1 sprig of basil. Serve immediately. Serves 6.

Italian Vegetable Medley

2 large carrots
l large red onion
l medium red bell pepper
l medium green bell pepper
2 medium zucchini
2 medium yellow squash
1/2 stick butter

1/4 cup olive oil
2 tablespoons chopped
  garlic clove
1/2 tablespoon black pepper,
  freshly ground
Salt to taste

Wash all vegetables. Peel carrots and onions, and seed peppers. Julienne all vegetables. Heat butter, oil, and garlic over medium heat; sauté vegetables until tender. Add spices. Serves 6.

Chicken Florentine Roberto

2 pounds chicken breast,
  skinned and julienned
1 cup seasoned flour
6 ounces olive oil
32 ounces heavy cream

12 ounces spinach, chopped
l ounce chicken base
8 ounces Parmesan cheese
8 ounces sun-dried tomatoes
Cooked linguine

Dust chicken with flour and sauté until brown. Drain and remove from heat.

In large sauté pan, add 20 ounces heavy cream and spinach. Cook until thickened and reduce heat. In a separate pan, add chicken base and remaining cream; dissolve over medium heat. Pour chicken base mixture into spinach and cream, add chicken, Parmesan cheese, and sun-dried tomatoes. After cheese has melted, add cooked linguine. Simmer l minute and serve. Serves 6 to 8.

Veal Zefferino

1 1/2 pounds veal scallopini
  (2 2-ounce slices per person)
3 tablespoons garlic clove,
  chopped
Olive oil or salad oil
1 1/2 cups fresh mushrooms,
  sliced

1 1/2 cups walnut pieces
1 1/2 cups white wine
1/2 teaspoon salt
1/2 teaspoon black pepper
6 ounces demi-glaze
6 ounces heavy cream
1 tablespoon parsley, chopped

Sauté veal slices and garlic in oil over high heat for 2 minutes (1 minute per side). Add mushrooms, walnuts, and white wine. Season with salt and pepper. Add demi-glaze and cream; reduce until sauce thickens. Stir in parsley. Remove from heat and serve. Serves 6.

Cassata D'Amato's

1 pound cake
1 pound ricotta cheese
2 egg yolks
2 tablespoons heavy cream
1/4 cup sugar

3 tablespoons Frangelico liqueur
2 tablespoons lemon zest
4 ounces grated
  semi-sweet chocolate
Chocolate Coffee Icing*

Cut 1/4 inch off each end of the pound cake and discard. Cut cake horizontally into 4 long, even slices.

In blender, combine ricotta cheese, egg yolks, heavy cream, sugar, and liqueur. Blend until smooth. Slowly add in lemon zest and chocolate. Divide mixture into 3 even portions. Place 1 slice of pound cake on serving tray. Evenly cover the slice of cake with 1/3 of ricotta mixture. Repeat with second and third slices of pound cake, using all the ricotta mixture. Wrap cake and refrigerate for 2 hours to firm cake.

Chocolate Coffee Icing:
3 ounces unsweetened chocolate
3 tablespoons butter
1/8 teaspoon salt
1/4 cup hot water

1 teaspoon instant coffee
2 cups powdered sugar
1 teaspoon vanilla

Melt chocolate and butter over low heat. Add salt and remove from heat. Mix water and coffee, add to chocolate mixture. Gradually add sugar and vanilla. Pour mixture into mixing bowl and beat until creamy, using a wire whip. Spread on cake.

August Moon

I*f you love Chinese food, or if you just like Chinese food, or even if you have never tasted Chinese food - you really should go directly to August Moon! This is a restaurant where the meal is prepared so delightfully that you become an instant fan.*

At August moon, beauty and palatability go hand in hand. Each serving is freshly-cooked, decoratively arranged on the plate, and arrives at the table like a piping-hot work of art.

Pauline and Fu-Tsun Lin own and manage August Moon. The Lins, originally from Taiwan, have been married almost three years, and share an enthusiasm for the restaurant business. Mr. Lin was trained by famous chefs in Taiwan and Japan, and spends most of his time preparing the marvelous dishes, while Mrs. Lin prefers to take care of business and greeting customers. They own restaurants in Richmond and Nashville too, but like making their home in Lexington.

Such masterful creations as Prawns and Crab with Garlic Sauce, Uncle Lin's Chicken, and August Moon Sizzling Seafood ensure a return visit, and the striking dining room makes the visit a pleasant one. With seating for 200, the shiny black chairs and dark cloths blend softly with mauve-toned carpeting and elegant Chinese glass panels. The dining room is much more beautiful than the exterior indicates.

If you would like the Lins to cater a party or dinner off premises, they will do so gladly - for as many as you like. Whenever or wherever you dine with the Lins, you will enjoy Chinese cuisine the way it was meant to be served.

Owners: Pauline and Fu - Tsu Lin
Address: 2690 Nicholasville Road
Lexington, Kentucky 40503
Telephone: (606) 277-8888 or (606) 277-8393
Hours & Days: Monday-Thursday 11:00 am to 10:00 pm
Friday 11:00 am to 11:00 pm
Saturday 12:00 noon to 11:00 pm
Sunday 12:00 noon to 10:00 pm
Reservations recommended
Visa, MasterCard, American Express
Directions: Nicholasville Road at New Circle

Polynesian Drinks & Cocktails

1. **HOUSE SPECIAL DRINK** ... 3.95
   Our lovable drink. Combination of white rum, orange juice, pineapple juice and our bar tender's secret special mix, topped with Bacardi 151, it will give you a fantastic feeling.

2. **MAI TAI** 3.75
   A famous mixture of rums and Mai Tai mix. It's an excellent drink.

3. **ZOMBIE** 3.75
   Two kings of rums blended with favorite fruit mix, add apricot brandy, then topped with Bacardi 151, brings you to a great feeling.

4. **HURRICANE SUSIE** 3.50
   A blending of white rum, orange curacao, gin and pineapple juice. It will accompany you till the storm passes.

5. **PINA COLADA** 3.95
   A delightful drink, blending rum, pineapple juice with the real cream of fresh sun-ripened Caribbean coconut.

6. **FOG CUTTER** 3.95
   It's a combination of rum, gin, brandy, Tiki mix, it will help you make it through the night.

7. **FLAMING VOLCANO** 6.95
   (For Two.)
   An eruption of the finest rums fired with sacred nectars.

8. **SCORPIO** 3.95
   A blending of rum, orange curaco, Tiki mix. It will bring you a fitting climax to an incomparable dinner.

9. **LONG ISLAND TEA** 3.95
   An incomparable drink, consisting of rum, gin, vodka, triple sec and sour mix. It has powerful strength.

10. **JUMBO FROZEN DAIQUIRI** 3.95
    With pineapple, banana or straw-berry.

11. **FORBIDDEN JUNGLE** 3.50
    Rums, pineapple juice, orange juice with coconut.

12. **BLUE HAWAIIAN** 3.50
    A delightful drink, blending rum and tropical fruits.

13. **NAVY GROG** 3.75
    Famous for its special witches blend of brew, Barbados and Haitian Rums.

14. **PASSION PUNCH** 3.75
    A delightful drink of La Grande passion with orange, pineapple juice.

Cocktails

BAR BRAND 2.75
Whiskey Sour, Martini, Gimlet, Manhattan, Screw Driver, Tom Collins, etc.

CALL BRAND 2.95
Jack Daniels, Maker's Mark, Early Time, Old Charter, Wild Turkey, Smirnoff, Canadian Club, Canadian Mist, Seagrams 7, Seagrams V.O., Crown Royal, J&B, Cutty Sark, Dewars, Chivas Regal, Beefeater, Tanqueray, Bombay, etc.
ABSOLUTE, STOLICHNAYA, JOHNNIE BLACK 3.25

AFTER DINNER DRINKS 3.25
Irish Coffee, Grand Marnier, Tia Maria, B&B, Drambuie, Kahlua, Amaretto, Bailey's Irish Cream, etc.
HENNESSEY, COGNAC, COURVOISIER, REMY MARTIN 3.50

Wine List

Oriental Wines

			Bottle
FRENCH WAN FU .... (½ Bottle)	5.50		11.00
JAPANESE SAKE .... (Split)	4.75		11.00
JAPANESE PLUM WINE .... (Split)	4.75		9.00

Selected House Wine
CALIFORNIA CELLAR
Chablis, Rose, Burgundy
Glass $1.50   ½ Carafe $4.00
Carafe $7.00

WHITE ZINFANDEL
Glass $2.25   ½ Carafe $5.50
Carafe $10.50

Champagnes

MARTINI ROSSI ASTI SPUMANTE	15.50
KOBEL BRUT	22.00
TAYLOR DRY CHAMPAGNE	11.50
LEJON WHITE OR PINK	9.50

White Wines

BLUE NUN	9.00
CHRISTIAN BROTHER CHABLIS	6.50
TAYLOR CHABLIS	7.50
BUENNA VISTA	9.00
CHARDONNAY	12.00

Rose Wines

MATEUS ROSE	8.50
LANCER ROSE	8.50
TAYLOR ROSE	7.50

Red Wines

BEAUJOLAIS-VILLAGES JADOT	9.50
RIUNITE LAMBRUSCO	8.95
TAYLOR BURGUNDY	7.50

After Dinner Wines

HARVEY'S BRISTOL CREAM (Glass)	2.25
DUBONNET RED (Glass)	2.00
CREAM SHERRY (Glass)	2.00

Beers

IMPORTED: HEINEKEN, KIRIN, TSING TAO, CORONA 2.25
DOMESTIC: MILLER LITE, BUDWEISER, MICHELOB LITE,
MICHELOB, COORS, COORS LITE, BUD LITE   1.75

August Moon Dinner

*Served with Crabmeat & Chicken Corn Soup, Volcano Plate,
Fried Rice, Hot Tea and Fourtune Cookies.*

The following selections are recommended but the privilege
of choosing any other dishes is extended.

CHOICE OF ONE PER PERSON — $19.95 PER PERSON

309 HAPPY FAMILY
302 SESAME CHICKEN
★314 TRIPLE CROWN
     MANDARIN STYLE
501 PEKING DUCK
306 KING'S THREE IN ONE

★316 AUGUST MOON SEAFOOD
     SPLENDOR
305 FOUR HAPPINESS
★318 BEEF & SHRIMP DELIGHT
317 AUGUST MOON SIZZLING
     SEAFOOD

Appetizers

火焰拼盤   **101. VOLCANO PLATE** 7.90
*Appetizers for two including egg rolls, sa cha beef, shrimp toast, jumbo fried
shrimp, sesame chicken wings and spareribs. Additional person $3.95 each.*

春捲   **102. EGG ROLL** 1.10
Crispy, golden brown with vegetables, pork and shrimp.

蝦吐司   **103. SHRIMP TOAST (4)** 3.50
Minced shrimp and water chestnuts fried with bread.

蜜汁排骨   **104. HONEY-CURED BAR-B-Q SPARERIBS (4)** 4.25

沙茶牛肉串   **105. CHO CHO (4)** 4.25
Sliced bar-b-q beef marinated with sa cha sauce on fire pot.

芝蔴鷄翅   **106. CHICKEN WING WITH SESAME** 2.50
Golden fried chicken wings in chef's special sauce, topped with sesame.

炸雲吞   **107. CRISPY WONTON (6)** 2.00

炸大蝦   **108. FRIED JUMBO SHRIMP (4)** 3.25

鍋貼   **109. FRIED DUMPLINGS (6)** 3.95

蒸餃   **110. STEAMED DUMPLINGS (6)** 3.95

蟹餃   **111. CRAB RANGOON (6)** 3.95
Cream cheese with crab meat and spices in wonton wrap and deep fried.

Soup

雲吞湯   **201. WONTON SOUP** 1.00

蛋花湯   **202. EGG FLOWER SOUP** .... .95

酸辣湯 ★**203. HOT AND SOUR SOUP** 1.10

三鮮湯   **204. SAN HSIEN SOUP (2)** 3.50
Beef, shrimp and chicken with vegetables.

海鮮鍋巴湯   **205. SIZZLING SEAFOOD SOUP (2)** 4.75
Crabmeat, lobster, scallops and shrimp with snow peas, mushrooms in a delicate soup.

蔬菜豆腐湯   **206. BEAN CURD VEGETABLE SOUP (2)** 3.25

龍鳳湯   **207. CRABMEAT & CHICKEN CORN SOUP** 4.75

> **WE CATER TO GROUPS OF ALL SIZES.
> PRIVATE PARTY ROOM AVAILABLE.**

There will be a minimum charge of $5.00 per person.

A 15% gratuity will be added on parties of 6 or more.

★ *HOT & SPICY. WE CAN ALTER THE SPICE ACCORDING TO YOUR TASTE.*

August Moon Banquet

*With a national reputation of experience in
banquets, our host and chef will make sure you and
your guests have an unforgettable evening.
Give us a one day notice and the rest is just magic.*

MINIMUM OF EIGHT PERSONS — $20.00 UP PER PERSON

Deluxe Family Dinner

*Served with Egg Roll, Shrimp Toast, Sesame Chicken Wing
and Choice of Soup (Wonton, Egg Flower or Hot & Sour),
Fried Rice, Hot Tea and Fortune Cookies.*

CHOICE OF ONE PER PERSON — $14.95 PER PERSON

312	PHOENIX & DRAGON WITH CASHEWS	313	CHOW SAN SHIEN
★703	FIVE FLAVORED SHRIMP	★318	BEEF AND SHRIMP DELIGHT
502	CRISPY DUCK	302	SESAME CHICKEN
601	TROUT DELIGHT	304	TERIYAKI STEAK
★320	HONG KONG LAMB	307	WONDERFUL SWEET & SOUR

August Moon Specialties

(Served with Egg Fried Rice, Hot Tea and Fortune Cookies.)

雀巢鷄 **301. CHICKEN IN BIRD'S NEST** **10.25**
Sliced chicken sauteed with fresh zucchini, mushrooms and roasted black walnuts in chef's special sauce, served in a golden brown potato string nest.

芝麻鷄 **302. SESAME CHICKEN** **10.25**
Golden fried chicken sauteed in chef's special honey-lemon sauce, then generously sprinkled with sesame.

林厨鷄 **★303. UNCLE LIN'S CHICKEN** **10.25**
Fried chicken chunks sauteed with fresh zucchini, sweet red peppers and bamboo shoot in chef's very own hot sauce. One of August Moon's very special creations.

火燒牛排 **304. TERIYAKI STEAK** **11.25**
Tender filet mignon marinated with chef's special teriyaki sauce and sauteed with assorted vegetables served on a sizzling plate. An exotic dish.

四喜 **305. FOUR HAPPINESS** **11.95**
Shrimp, beef, pork and lamb sauteed with snow peas, bamboo shoots & other Chinese vegetables in chef's special brown sauce.

三冠王 **306. KING'S THREE IN ONE** **13.65**
Lobster, filet mignon and chicken sauteed with fresh zucchini, broccoli, corn and mushroom in chef's special brown sauce.

甜酸總會 **307. WONDERFUL SWEET AND SOUR** **9.55**
Shrimp, chicken and pork, deep fried and topped with vegetables and special sweet & sour sauce.

魚香羊 **★308. FIVE FLAVORED LAMB** **9.95**
Sliced tender lamb sauteed with fresh mushrooms, zucchini, snow peas & other Chinese vegetables in hot five flavored sauce.

全家福 **309. HAPPY FAMILY** **12.95**
Lobster, crabmeat, scallops, steak, chicken and pork sauteed with fresh zucchini, mushrooms, snow peas and other Chinese vegetables in chef's special brown sauce. Shrimp

核桃蝦球 **310. WALNUT SHRIMP** **10.55**
Jumbo shrimp sauteed with fresh mushrooms, zucchini & other vegetables in a tantalizing tomato based sauce & then topped with honey roasted black walnuts.

蒜爆蝦蟹 **★311. PRAWNS AND CRABS WITH GARLIC SAUCE** **13.95**
Delicately white-wine marinated prawns and king crab meat sauteed with fresh vegetables in garlic sauce.

腰菓雙柳 **312. PHOENIX AND DRAGON WITH CASHEWS** **10.55**
Fresh zucchini, mushrooms, snow peas and other Chinese vegetables sauteed with shrimp and chicken in chef's special white sauce.

炒三鮮 **313. CHOW SAN SIEN** **10.55**
Shrimp, chicken and beef sauteed with broccoli, bamboo shoots and other vegetables in chef's special sauce.

魚香三鮮 **★314. TRIPLE CROWN MANDARIN STYLE** **10.55**
Shrimp, chicken, beef and Chinese vegetables sauteed with five-flavored sauce.

魚香海鮮牛 **★315. FIVE FLAVORED SEAFOOD AND STEAK** **13.95**
Lobster, king crab meat, shrimp, scallops, filet mignon are sauteed with fresh zucchini, mushrooms, snow peas and other Chinese vegetables in chef's special hot sauce.

魚香海鮮 **★316. AUGUST MOON SEAFOOD SPLENDOR** **13.95**
King crab meat, lobster, scallops and shrimp sauteed with fresh zucchini, mushrooms, snow peas and other Chinese vegetables in chef's special hot sauce.

海鮮鍋巴 **317. AUGUST MOON SIZZLING SEAFOOD** **13.95**
Listen to it snap and pop—a gourmet special full of lobster, shrimp, scallops, king crab meat and fresh vegetables.

爆兩樣 **★318. BEEF AND SHRIMP DELIGHT** **10.95**
Shrimp and choice tender beef sauteed with fresh vegetables in hot sauce.

葱爆羊 **319. MONGOLIAN LAMB** **9.95**
Green onions & Chinese vegetables sauteed with sliced tender lamb in chef's special sauce, topped with crispy rice noodles.

麻辣羊 **★320. HONG KONG LAMB** **9.95**
Fresh mushrooms and other vegetables sauteed with tender lamb in chef's special hot sauce.

★ HOT & SPICY. WE CAN ALTER THE SPICE ACCORDING TO YOUR TASTE.

七星伴月 **401. AUGUST MOON SURROUNDED BY SEVEN STARS
$20.95 FOR TWO**
*An experience to remember — for an extra ordinary evening!!!
A very unique, sumptuous meal specially prepared by our chief chef.
Lobster, crabmeat, scallops and shrimp with corn, zucchini, water chestnuts,
fresh mushrooms sauteed in our very own white sauce on the center of the plate
then surrounded by fried jumbo shrimp &* ~~crispy wonton.~~ *Crab Rangoon*

Duck

(Served with Fried Rice, Hot Tea and Fortune Cookies.)

北京鴨 **501. PEKING DUCK** .... (Whole) **23.00**
Duck Peking style served with pancakes, scallions and Hoisin sauce. (Half) **12.50**

香酥鴨 **502. CRISPY DUCK** **9.95**
Duck marinated on the bond in a special sauce, steamed, crispy fried to a golden brown, served with duck sauce. Truly for the gourmet.

杏仁鴨 **503. ALMOND DUCK** **9.95**
Golden fried boneless duckling topped with sliced almonds & sweet and sour sauce. It's crispy & tasty.

Fish

(Served with Fried Rice, Hot Tea and Fortune Cookies.)

乾煎鱒魚 **601. TROUT DELIGHT** **9.50**
Boneless trout simmered in chef's special sauce with fresh zucchini, mushrooms and other vegetables

Seafood

(Served with Fried Rice, Hot Tea and Fortune Cookies.)

沙茶蝦 **★701. SA CHA SHRIMP** **8.95**
Fresh zucchini, mushrooms and other Chinese vegetables sauteed with jumbo shrimp in sa cha sauce.

彩虹蝦 **702. RAINBOW SHRIMP** **8.95**
Fresh mushrooms, snow peas, zucchini and other Chinese vegetables sauteed with jumbo shrimp in light sauce.

魚香蝦 **★703. FIVE-FLAVORED SHRIMP** **8.95**
Shrimp sauteed with fresh mushrooms, zucchini, snow peas and other Chinese vegetables in hot five-flavored sauce.

雪豆蝦 **704. SHRIMP WITH SNOW PEAS** **8.95**
Fresh snow peas and other Chinese vegetables sauteed with jumbo shrimp in light sauce.

宮保蝦 **★705. GOVERNOR'S SHRIMP** **8.95**
Fresh celery and other Chinese vegetables sauteed with shrimp in fine hot sauce.

乾燒蝦 **★706. HONG KONG SHRIMP** **8.95**
Hot pepper sauce and minced water chestnuts, bamboo shoots and mushrooms are used to make a gourmet dish of shrimp.

蝦龍糊 **707. SHRIMP WITH LOBSTER SAUCE** **8.95**
Fresh mushrooms, carrots and other vegetables sauteed with shrimp in scrambled egg and lobster sauce.

甜酸蝦 **708. SWEET AND SOUR SHRIMP** **8.55**
Deep fried shrimp served with pineapple and carrots in freshly made sweet and sour sauce.

芥蘭蝦 **709. SHRIMP WITH BROCCOLI** **8.95**
Fresh broccoli sauteed with shrimp in light sauce.

腰菓蝦 **710. SHRIMP WITH CASHEW NUTS** **8.95**
Shrimp served with crispy cashew nuts, water chestnuts, green peas, carrots and mushrooms in white sauce.

明園干貝 **711. SCALLOPS DELIGHT** **9.25**
Fresh zucchini, corn, snow peas and other Chinese vegetables sauteed with scallops in light sauce.

魚香干貝 **★712. FIVE-FLAVORED SCALLOPS** **9.25**
Fresh zucchini, snow peas, mushrooms and other vegetables sauteed with scallops in hot five-flavored sauce.

```
╔════════════════════════════════════════╗
         Family Dinner
   Served with Egg Roll, Sesame Chicken Wing and
   Choice of Soup (Wonton, Egg Flower or Hot and Sour Soup),
        Fried Rice, Hot Tea and Fortune Cookies.

   CHOICE OF ONE PER PERSON — $10.95 PER PERSON
╚════════════════════════════════════════╝
```

1004 MONGOLIAN PORK	702 RAINBOW SHRIMP
★906 FIVE FLAVORED CHICKEN	709 SHRIMP WITH BROCCOLI
907 CASHEW CHICKEN	★803 GOVERNOR'S BEEF
809 BEEF WITH CHINESE VEGETABLES	905 MOO GOO GAI PAN
	★807 SA CHA BEEF

Beef

(Served with Fried Rice, Hot Tea and Fortune Cookies.)

青椒牛 801. **GREEN PEPPER STEAK** 7.55
Sliced tender beef sauteed with green pepper and other vegetables in brown sauce.

葱爆牛 802. **MONGOLIAN BEEF** 7.55
Green onion and Chinese vegetables sauteed with sliced tender beef in chef's special sauce.

宮保牛 ★803. **GOVERNOR'S BEEF** 7.75
Peanuts, fresh celery and green onions sauteed with tender beef in hot sauce.

雙冬牛 804. **BEEF DELIGHT** 7.95
Sliced tender beef sauteed with snow peas and other Chinese vegetables in special sauce.

芥蘭牛 805. **BEEF WITH BROCCOLI** 7.55
Fresh broccoli sauteed with tender sliced beef in brown sauce.

魚香牛 ★806. **FIVE-FLAVORED STEAK** 7.75
Sliced tender beef, fresh mushrooms sauteed in five-flavored sauce with Chinese vegetables.

沙茶牛 ★807. **SA CHA BEEF** 7.55
Sliced tender beef, fresh broccoli and mushrooms sauteed in sa cha sauce with Chinese vegetables.

雪豆牛 808. **BEEF WITH SNOW PEAS** 7.95
Fresh snow peas sauteed with sliced tender beef in chef's special sauce.

素菜牛 809. **BEEF WITH CHINESE VEGETABLES** 7.55
Fresh snow peas, mushrooms and other Chinese vegetables sauteed with tender sliced beef in brown sauce.

麻辣牛 ★810. **HONG KONG BEEF** 7.55
Fresh mushrooms and other vegetables sauteed with tenderloin in five-flavored sauce.

Chicken

(Served with Fried Rice, Hot Tea and Fortune Cookies.)

玉米鶏 901. **CHICKEN WITH BABY CORN** 7.25
Fresh zucchini, snow peas, baby corn sauteed with chicken in light sauce.

芥蘭鶏 902. **CHICKEN WITH BROCCOLI** 7.25
Sliced chicken sauteed with broccoli and water chestnuts in brown sauce.

雙冬鶏 903. **CHICKEN DELIGHT** 7.55
Sliced chicken sauteed with Chinese vegetables in brown sauce.

宮保鶏 904. **GOVERNOR'S CHICKEN** 7.55
Peanuts, fresh celery and green onions sauteed diced chicken in hot sauce.

蘑菇鶏 905. **MOO GOO GAI PAN** 7.25
Sliced chicken sauteed with water chestnuts and fresh mushrooms, carrots and broccoli in light sauce.

魚香鶏 ★906. **FIVE-FLAVORED CHICKEN** 7.55
Sliced chicken sauteed with Chinese vegetables in five-flavored sauce.

腰菓鶏 907. **CASHEW CHICKEN** 7.55
Chicken served with crispy cashew nuts, carrots, mushrooms and other vegetables in light sauce.

咖哩鶏 ★908. **CURRY CHICKEN** 7.25
Fresh onions tastefully matched with other Chinese vegetables and sauteed with chicken in chef's special curry sauce.

檸檬鶏 909. **LEMON CHICKEN** 7.25
Breaded tender chicken sauteed with chef's special lemon sauce.

杏仁鶏 910. **ALMOND CHICKEN** 7.25
Fresh mushrooms, celery, carrots and other Chinese vegetables sauteed with diced chicken in dark sauce showered with crispy almonds.

甜酸鶏 911. **SWEET AND SOUR CHICKEN** 7.25
Deep fried chicken topped with vegetables and fresh home made sweet and sour sauce.

八寶鶏 912. **EIGHT TREASURES CHICKEN** 7.25
Diced chicken and bar-b-q pork with mixed vegetables & peanuts in our own brown sauce.

紅燒鶏 913. **HONG SHU GAI** 7.25
Tender breaded chicken breast stir fried with fresh broccoli, snow peas & other vegetables in brown sauce.

★ *HOT & SPICY.*

Pork

(Served with Fried Rice, Hot Tea and Fortune Cookies.)

木須肉 1001. **MOO SHI PORK** 7.25
Pork strips sauteed with bamboo shoots and other vegetables, served with four pancakes and Hoisin sauce.

回鍋肉 ★1002. **TWICE COOKED PORK** 6.95
Pork slices dipped in sizzling oil, then sauteed with mushrooms and vegetables in hot sauce.

湘潭肉絲 ★1003. **PORK WITH BLACK BEAN SAUCE** 6.95
Pork strips sauteed with Chinese vegetables in hot black bean sauce.

葱爆肉絲 ★1004. **MONGOLIAN PORK** 6.95
Fresh green onions sauteed with pork strips, bamboo shoots, rice noodles in brown sauce.

魚香肉絲 ★1005. **FIVE-FLAVORED PORK** 6.95
Pork strips sauteed with bamboo shoots and other Chinese vegetables in hot sauce.

甜酸肉 1006. **SWEET AND SOUR PORK** 6.95
Deep fried pork chunks topped with vegetables and fresh home made sweet and sour sauce.

麻婆豆腐 ★1007. **SPICY FORMOSA BEAN CURD** 5.75
Bean curd sauteed with special hot sauce.

魚香茄子 ★1008. **FIVE-FLAVORED EGGPLANT** 5.75
Eggplant sauted with minced pork in dark sauce.

家常豆腐 1009. **BEAN CURD FAMILY STYLE** 5.75
Bean curd and pork sauteed with chef's special sauce.

Vegetables

(Served with Fried Rice, Hot Tea and Fortune Cookies.)

炒三冬 1101. **AUGUST MOON DELIGHT** 6.95
Black mushrooms, bamboo shoots and fresh mushrooms sauteed in light sauce.

雪豆馬蹄 1102. **SNOW PEAS DELIGHT** 6.95
Fresh snow peas are tastefully balanced with other vegetables in light sauce.

素什錦 1103. **VEGETARIAN'S PARADISE** 6.95
Fresh broccoli, green peppers, carrots and snow peas and other Chinese vegetables sauteed in light sauce.

羅漢齋 1104. **BUDDHIST DELIGHT** 6.95
Fresh mushrooms, snow peas, broccoli and other Chinese vegetables sauteed with fried bean curd in light sauce.

Chow Mein & Chop Suey

(Served with Fried Rice, Hot Tea and Fortune Cookies.)

炒麵 1201. **CHOW MEIN** (Chicken, Pork, Beef) 5.95
蝦炒麵 1202. **SHRIMP or COMBINATION CHOW MEIN** 6.95
雜碎 1203. **CHOW SUEY** (Chicken, Pork, Beef) 5.95
蝦雜碎 1204. **SHRIMP or COMBINATION CHOP SUEY** 6.95
撈麵 1205. **CHINESE SOFT NOODLES** (Chicken, Pork, Beef) 5.95
蝦撈麵 1206. **SHRIMP or COMBINATION SOFT NOODLES** 6.95

Egg Foo Young & Fried Rice

芙蓉蛋 1301. **EGG FOO YOUNG** (Chicken, Pork or Beef) 6.55
蝦芙蓉蛋 1302. **SHRIMP EGG FOO YOUNG** 7.25
炒飯 1303. **FRIED RICE** (Chicken, Pork or Beef) 5.95
蝦炒飯 1304. **SHRIMP or COMBINATION FRIED RICE** 6.95

Desserts

ICE CREAM	1.25
HONEY BANANA (4)	2.95
HONEY APPLE (4)	2.95
ALMOND COOKIE	.35
LYCHEES	1.75

Beverages

PEPSI, MT. DEW, 7 UP	.85
MILK	.85
PERRIER	1.75
BOTTOMLESS ICE TEA or COFFEE	.85
JUICES: ORANGES, CRANBERRY, GRAPFRUIT	.85

Vegetable Paradise

4 teaspoons cooking oil
2 cloves garlic,
  peeled and mashed
2 stalks broccoli,
  cut into 5 pieces each
1/2 green pepper,
  cut into 1-inch cubes
1 baby carrot, cut into 6 slices
6 snow peas, strings removed
1/2 zucchini,
  cut into 1/2-inch diagonal slices
1 small onion, slivered

1/2 red pepper,
  cut into 1-inch cubes
3 medium mushrooms,
  quartered lengthwise
2 nappa cabbage leaves,
  cut into 1-inch squares
1/2 small can sliced
  water chestnuts
1 pinch salt
1 teaspoon cooking wine
2 teaspoons cornstarch
4 teaspoons cold water
Steamed rice

Heat wok for 3 minutes before adding oil to prevent food from sticking. Pour oil into wok and wait for bubbles to form. Add garlic and stir-fry until brown. Add all vegetables at once and stir-fry 6 minutes. Be careful not to overcook or vegetable crispness will be lost. Thoroughly mix cornstarch into water, then add to stir-fried vegetables in wok. Stir once. Serve with steamed rice. Serves 2.

Rainbow Shrimp

12 jumbo shrimp,
  peeled and deveined
4 teaspoons cornstarch
4 teaspoons cooking oil
1/2 medium zucchini,
  cut into 1/2-inch diagonal slices
1/2 red bell pepper,
  cut into 1-inch squares
2 nappa cabbage leaves,
  cut into 1-inch squares

4 medium mushrooms,
  quartered lengthwise
6 snow peas, strings removed
1/3 teaspoon salt
1 pinch black pepper
1/2 teaspoon sugar
4 teaspoons cold water
Steamed rice

Heat wok for 3 minutes to prevent food from sticking. Cover shrimp thoroughly with 2 teaspoons cornstarch. Add cooking oil to wok and heat until bubbles form. Add shrimp and stir-fry 4 minutes. Add vegetables and stir-fry with shrimp. Add salt, pepper, and sugar. Mix together remaining cornstarch and cold water. Add to wok and stir. Serve with steamed rice. Serves 2.

Bombay Indian Restaurant

Bombay Indian Restaurant is the dream of the Rao family from India, and a dream come true for those of us who love wonderful Indian cuisine.

Located on the second floor of Chevy Chase Place, Bombay Indian's clean, cool gray walls and black and white tiles are a crisp, lively contrast to the enticing sitar music and exotic flavors awaiting you. If you thought Indian food was only curry powder and chutney, you are in for a nice surprise and a wonderful meal. As you will discover, there are roasted meats, flaky pastries, fabulous vegetable concoctions and great desserts.

Though the Rao family is from southern India, they serve foods from all parts of the country. Mutter Paneer, a delightful dish of peas and cheese, is from Punjab and Lamb Curry (Korma) is part of a traditional North India Buffet Banquet. The owners work happily together in all aspects of the restaurant from greeting to cooking, and helpful waiters make ordering so easy for even the novice.

Most of us in this part of the country have never had the opportunity to experience Indian food prepared so exquisitely. Judging from the crowds at Bombay Indian Restaurant, Lexington realizes its good fortune!

Owners: Raghu Rao and Murali Rao
Address: 824 Euclid Avenue
          Suite 204, Chevy Chase Plaza
          Lexington, Kentucky 40502
Telephone: (606) 266-6221
Hours & Days: Lunch: Monday-Friday 11:00 am to 2:00 pm
               Dinner: Monday-Friday 5:00 pm to 9:00 pm
                       Saturday 12:00 noon to 9:00 pm
               Closed Sundays
Reservations recommended
Free parking available
MasterCard, Visa, American Express, Diner's Club
Directions: Second floor of the Chevy Chase Plaza
             on the corner of Euclid and East High.

STARTERS

1.	VEGETABLE SAMOSA	— Triangular patties with seasoned vegetable stuffing . . . . $	2.15
2.	BEEF SAMOSA	— Triangular patties with mildly spiced minced beef filling . . . . $	2.15
3.	PAKORA	— Onion fritters spiced to taste just right . . . . $	1.95
4.	PAPPAD	— Delicately spiced wafer thin lentil crackers . . . . $	.85

MEAT DELIGHTS

5.	CHICKEN KURMA	— Boneless pieces of chicken, cooked in yogurt, sauce and spices . . . . . . $	7.65
6.	LAMB CURRY	— A curry of lamb cooked with onions, tomatoes and coriander . . . . $	7.35
7.	TANDOORI CHICKEN	— Chicken marinated in yogurt, garlic, ginger and many other secret . . . $ spices, then baked in the oven.	7.45
8.	BEEF VINDALOO	— A curry of beef cooked with special spices . . . . $	7.65

VEGETARIAN DELIGHTS

9.	MIXED VEGETABLE CURRY	— Seasoned vegetables in the village style, prepared with a touch of . . . . $ spices and herbs.	5.95
10.	ALOO GOBI	— Cauliflower and potatos in a piquant blend of spices . . . . $	5.90
11.	CHANNA MASALA	— Gorbanzo beans cooked with special herbs and spices . . . . $	5.85
12.	MUTTER PANEER	— Green peas cooked with home made cottage cheese and delicately . . . . $ seasoned.	6.15

INDIAN BREADS

13. POORI — Soft fluffy whole wheat bread deep fried in pure vegetable oil . . . . . . $_____ 1.95

14. CHAPATHI — Whole wheat flour bread baked on a griddle . . . . $_____ 1.25

15. NAAN — Leavened bread of fine flour . . . . $_____ .95

16. ALOO PARATHA — Multi layered whole wheat bread stuffed with delicately seasoned . . . . $_____ 2.15
mashed potatos

RICE DELIGHTS

17. CHICKEN BIRYANI — Tender pieces of chicken cooked with long grain rice . . . . $_____ 8.35

18. VEGETABLE PULAV — Basumathi rice cooked with garden fresh vegetables and exotic . . . . . . $_____ 6.95
spices.

19. PLAIN RICE — Steam cooked long grain rice . . . . $_____ 1.35

*PLAIN RICE with DHAALL — Steam cooked long grain rice with Dhaall . . . . $_____ 2.20

DESSERTS

20. GULAB JAMUN — Fried cheese balls soaked in saffron and rose flavored syrup . $_____ 2.15

21. RASMALAI — Cottage cheese in sweetened condensed milk . . . . $_____ 2.15
flavored and sauteed with nuts

22. KESAR-PISTA ICE CREAM — Special kind of ice cream made with saffron and pistachios . . . . $_____ 1.95

SIDE ORDERS:

CHUTNEY . . . . $_____ .60   RAITA . . . . $_____ .95

DINNER SPECIALS

(Thalis represent a traditional full course meal.)

23. * VEGETARIAN THALI * — Pappad, two vegetable curries, vegetable pulau, pickles, 2-pooris, ... $_____ 14.85
Samosa, and a dessert.

24. *NON-VEGETARIAN THALI* — Pappad, meat curry, Tandoori chicken, Biryani, pickles, 2-pooris, ... $_____ 15.65
Samosa, and a dessert.

Minced Lamb Meatballs
Stuffed with Almonds in Curry Sauce

16 whole unsalted
  blanched almonds
Boiling water
1 pound lean lamb,
  boneless, minced twice
1 egg
2 ounces besan*
1/2 teaspoon salt
1/4 teaspoon freshly
  ground black pepper
1 1/2 tablespoons water
Vegetable oil for deep frying
6 tablespoons ghee**

2 ounces onions, finely chopped
1 teaspoon garlic, finely chopped
2 1/2 teaspoons fresh ginger root,
  scraped and finely chopped
1/2 teaspoon ground coriander
1/2 teaspoon ground cumin
1/2 teaspoon turmeric
1/4 teaspoon cayenne pepper
3/8 pint plain yogurt
1/2 teaspoon garam masala*
  (see recipe, below)
1 1/2 tablespoons fresh coriander,
  finely chopped

Place almonds in boiling water for 2 hours, being careful that water covers almonds by 1 inch. Drain and discard water. Place lamb, egg, 1 ounce besan, salt, and pepper into a deep bowl. Knead vigorously, then beat with a spoon until smooth. Divide into 16 equal portions and shape each one into a meatball. Flatten each meatball into a circle, place 1 almond in center, and reshape into a meatball. Make a thick, smooth batter with remaining ounce of besan and 1 1/2 tablespoons water. Spread batter over each meatball with brush. Arrange on sheet of wax paper. Pour 3/4 pint oil into large pan or wok. Heat oil to 375 degrees. Deep fry meatballs, 5 or 6 at a time, turning frequently, for 5 minutes until golden brown. Transfer meatballs to plate when browned. Heat ghee in heavy saucepan. Add onions, garlic, and ginger, and stir 2 minutes. Add coriander, cumin, turmeric, and cayenne. Cook 10 minutes until onions are golden brown. Watch carefully for burning. Stir in yogurt, mix thoroughly, and add meatballs. Turn to coat and sprinkle with garam masala. Cover and simmer 10 minutes. Remove from heat. Let meatballs rest, covered, for 1 hour in sauce. Just before serving, simmer 5 minutes, stirring gently until hot. Sprinkle with fresh coriander and serve. Serves 4.

*Flour made by grinding chick-peas

**Butter oil made by cooking butter over low heat for 45 minutes. Clarified butter may be substituted.

Garam Masala:
5 3-inch pieces stick cinnamon
1 cup cardamom seeds
1/2 cup whole cloves

1/2 cup whole cumin seeds
1/4 cup whole coriander seeds
1/2 cup whole black peppercorns

Roast in 200-degree oven 30 minutes. Crush cinnamon sticks. Mix and grind all ingredients together to form a powder. Store. Makes 1 1/2 cups.

Boone Tavern

Barely forty miles from downtown Lexington lies Berea, the home of Berea College, numerous arts and crafts festivals, music fests, museums, and The Boone Tavern Hotel. A lovely drive through gently rolling bluegrass, white plank fences, and Kentucky horse farms is bound to soothe your nerves and stir your appetite. There is no better way to satisfy your hunger than with classic Kentucky cuisine from the Boone Tavern itself.

Boone Tavern, named in honor of Daniel Boone, is owned by the College and staffed by students in the hotel management program. The service is exemplary, with students offering hot bread, cleaning plates, refreshing your drink, and checking to make sure customers are happy.

The multi-coursed meal begins with a relish tray from which to choose such Southern delicacies as watermelon pickles or tiny marinated carrots. Next comes a hot bowl full of spoon bread. Boone Tavern is famous for this fluffy cornmeal soufflé, and it is delicious with any main dish. Following the spoon bread is your choice of many outstanding Southern offerings from Chicken Flakes in a Bird's Nest, Country Ham with Red Eye Gravy, Pan Fried Brook Trout, and, of course, Southern Fried Chicken. Dessert could be a local sweet-tooth satisfier such as Jefferson Davis Pie, served with homemade vanilla custard ice cream.

A brisk walk would be a welcome finale for a Boone Tavern feast, and there is plenty to see, as Boone Tavern is located right in the midst of the 125 year old Berea College campus. You'll find fine furniture, woven items, toys, brooms, ceramic, and wrought iron products crafted by Berea students. Visitors are invited to watch them being made, and many are offered for sale.

Your visit to Boone Tavern provides a unique opportunity to share the cultural and artistic heritage of the Appalacian Mountain Region and to enjoy a distinctively Southern dining experience.

Owner: Berea College
Address: CPO 2345, Main and Prospect Streets, Berea, Kentucky 40404
Telephone: (606) 986-9358
Hours & Days: Breakfast: 7:00 am to 9:00 am daily
               Lunch: Monday-Saturday 11:30 am to 1:30 pm
                        Sundays and Holidays 12:00 noon to 2:00 pm
               Dinner: 6:00 pm to 7:30 pm daily
Reservations recommended
Visa, MasterCard, American Express, Diner's Club, Discover, Carte Blanche
Directions: 40 miles south of Lexington on I-75. Take Exit 76 or 77 at
               Berea and follow signs to Berea College and Boone Tavern.

BREAKFAST OFFERINGS

Baker's offerings

Mary Liza's Sweet Roll

Rolled up with cinnamon sugar and pecans, glazed and served piping hot!

1.95

Country Biscuits

Two light, tender biscuits served up with whipped honey butter.

1.25

with sausage gravy 2.00

Muffin of the Day

At the whim of the baker, we make blueberry, bran, banana and corn muffins.

1.95

On the Side

Homefries with sweet onion	.95
Fried Apples	1.25
Sausage pan gravy	.95
Country Ham	1.95
Sausage Patties (2)	1.50
Bacon (3)	1.50
City Ham	1.50
Toast	.75

Experience...The Kentucky Breakfast
Authentic Country Ham, with our
chunky homefries and toast, served up
with fried apples and 1 egg any style.
Complete with juice and coffee.

5.75

Cereals

Oatmeal - 1.50   Grits - .85

Assorted Cold Cereal - 1.25

with sliced banana - 1.95

From the Griddle

Farmer's Breakfast

4 strips of bacon, with 2 "Sunny side up" eggs smack in the middle, served with toast.

3.50

Farm Fresh Eggs

Any way you like 'em, served with hominy grits and buttered toast.

One - 1.50   Two - 1.90

Pecan Pancakes

With maple butter and syrup

2.95

Southern Brancakes

Try this with honey & butter!

2.75

Beverages

Juices: Orange, Grapefruit, Tomato, Prune, Cranberry, Apple, Grape .95

Coffee, Tea, Milk or Decaffeinated Coffee .95

Saturday Dinner

All entrées include breads, salad, choice of appetizer, two vegetables, dessert and beverages.
A five percent sales tax will be added. Minimum charge is $5.50.

∞∞

ΔCREAM OF ONION SOUP

Fresh Fruit Cup   Wassail Punch

∞∞

*MOLDED BLACK CHERRY SALAD

∞∞

Country Relishes   *SOUTHERN SPOONBREAD   *DINNER ROLLS

∞∞

Entrées

1.	Roast Leg of Lamb with Caper Gravy and øMINT JELLY	$16.00
1.	*CHICKEN FLAKES with *SOUTHERN DRESSING	$12.75
2.	ΔSOUTHERN FRIED CHICKEN with *TAVERN HUSH PUPPY	$13.25
1.	Pan Fried Country Ham with Red Eye Gravy and Hominy Grits	$14.00
1.	Roast Kentucky Turkey, *SOUTHERN DRESSING & GIBLET GRAVY	$12.95
1.	Pan Fried Mountain Brook Trout, *TARTAR SAUCE	$14.25
1.	Pot Roast of Beef with *BUTTERED NOODLES	$14.25
	Three Vegetable Plate with Cottage Cheese	$9.00
	Child's Portion of the Above (under 12 years of age)	$5.50
	Extra Plate for a Child	$3.00

∞∞

Vegetables

1. øCHIVE BUTTERED NEW POTATO   4. Summer Squash
2. Green Beans   5. ΔPINEAPPLE BEETS
3. Corn Pudding   6. øKENTUCKY FRIED APPLES

∞∞

Desserts

Pumpkin Nut Roll   øNORWEGIAN CREAM CAKE

Apple Crisp A la mode   English Walnut Pie

ICE CREAMS FROM THE BOONE TAVERN KITCHEN:

Orange Sherbet   Blueberry Ice Cream

∞∞

Beverages

Milk   Buttermilk   Tea   Soft Drinks   Coffee   Decaf

∞∞

THESE RECIPES ARE FOUND IN R.T. HOUGEN'S COOKBOOKS
Δ COOKING WITH HOUGEN
✱ LOOK NO FURTHER   ⊙ MORE HOUGEN FAVORITES
PLEASE, NO TIPPING

Broccoli Roquefort Soup

1/4 cup flour
2 tablespoons chicken fat
 or butter
3 cups chicken stock
 or bouillon cubes

1 pint of milk
2 cups cooked broccoli, puréed
1/4 cup Roquefort cheese, grated

Make a roux by cooking flour with chicken fat for 2 minutes, stirring constantly. Add chicken stock and milk. Cook 5 minutes. Add puréed broccoli and grated cheese. Blend well. Serves 6.

Ruby Punch

2 16-ounce cans strained
 cranberry sauce
1 quart apple juice

Juice of 2 oranges
Juice of 1 lemon

Mix all ingredients and blend well with wire whisk. Bring to a boil. Serve hot. May also be served as a chilled punch. Serves 12 to 14.

Boone Tavern Cornsticks

1/2 cup flour
2 cups white cornmeal
1/2 teaspoon salt
1 teaspoon baking powder

1/2 teaspoon baking soda
2 cups buttermilk
2 eggs, well beaten
4 tablespoons melted lard

Sift flour, cornmeal, salt, and baking powder together. Mix soda and buttermilk, add to dry ingredients and beat well. Add eggs and beat. Add lard and mix well. Pour into well-greased, smoking hot cornstick pans on top of stove. Fill pans to level. Bake on lower shelf of oven at 450 to 500 degrees for 8 minutes. Move to upper shelf and bake 5 to 10 minutes longer. It is important to heat well-greased cornstick pans to smoking hot on top of stove before pouring in your batter. Makes 12 large cornsticks.

Southern Spoon Bread

1 1/4 cups white cornmeal
3 cups milk
3 eggs

1 teaspoon salt
1 3/4 teaspoons baking powder
2 tablespoons butter, melted

Stir meal into rapidly-boiling milk. Cook until very thick, stirring constantly, to prevent scorching. Remove from fire and allow to cool. The mixture will be cold and very stiff. Beat eggs; add to mixture along with salt, baking powder, and melted butter. Beat for 15 minutes. Pour into 2 well-greased casseroles. Bake at 375 degrees for 30 minutes. Serve from casseroles by spoonfuls. Serves 8 to 10.

Chicken Flakes in Bird's Nest

4 medium-size Idaho potatoes
5 cups Chicken Cream Sauce*

4 cups cooked chicken, diced
Deep fat for French frying

Peel and grate, or shred, potatoes. Line a strainer (4 inch diameter at top) with the shredded potatoes, using only enough to thinly cover inside of strainer. Place another strainer (2 inch diameter at top) inside first strainer, which will keep potatoes in place.

Place strainer in hot fat and fry until golden brown. Remove from fat, and tap potato nest with knife to loosen from strainer. Allow to cool and reheat in oven before serving the chicken flakes in the shell.

Combine chicken flakes and cream sauce. Add additional seasonings, if desired, and serve in bird nest. Serves 8.

*Chicken Cream Sauce:
6 tablespoons chicken fat
   or margarine

6 tablespoons sifted flour
3 cups chicken stock
Salt and pepper

Make a roux by mixing fat and flour in the top of a double boiler, cook for 5 minutes. Add hot chicken stock, stirring to prevent lumping. Season with salt and pepper. Serve over chicken.

Pork Chops, Some Tricky Way

4 lean pork chops
1/2 cup tomato paste
1/2 cup Parmesan cheese
1 cup bread crumbs

2 cups chicken stock
2 1/2 tablespoons flour
3/4 cup mushrooms, cut

Trim chops and brush with tomato paste. Mix Parmesan cheese with bread crumbs. Pat bread crumbs onto chops. Pan fry chops in a skillet until brown on both sides. Place chops in a covered casserole and add a small amount of water to prevent sticking. Bake at 350 degrees for 1 hour. Serve with a sauce made by thickening chicken stock with flour which has been smoothed to a paste with some of the cold stock. Cook for 5 minutes. Add mushrooms to the finished sauce. Serves 4.

Dessert

Jefferson Davis Pie

2 cups brown sugar
1 tablespoon flour, sifted
1/2 teaspoon nutmeg
1 cup cream
4 eggs, slightly beaten
1 teaspoon lemon juice

1/2 teaspoon lemon rind, grated
1/4 cup butter or margarine,
  melted
1 pie shell, unbaked
Whipped cream for topping

Sift sugar with flour and nutmeg; add cream, mixing well. Beat in eggs; add lemon juice, rind, and butter. Mix well. Pour into pie shell and bake at 375 degrees for 45 minutes. Cool, and serve with whipped cream. Serves 8.

Café on the Park

Café on the Park, located downtown in the Radisson Plaza Hotel, was named for its magnificent view of Triangle Park. The cascading fountains and seventy-seven pear trees in the park offer a tranquil and beautiful setting for dining that is unequaled in all of Lexington.

At Café on the Park, you may start the day off right with a delicious breakfast including many items from fresh fruit to Kentucky country ham and eggs. Many Lexington business people, as well as visitors, find the Café a pleasant and convenient stop for lunch. A multitude of mouth-watering dishes are on the lunch menu including their famous Vero Beach Cobb Salad, the traditional Kentucky Hot Brown, and Beer Cheese Soup. Dinner brings an even more sophisticated menu, but the same impeccable service. Cocktails and casual dining around a lovely bar built in the 1800's is also very popular with Lexingtonians.

The Radisson Hotel is noted for its attention to detail and its lush elegance. Café on the Park is no exception in both dining and atmosphere. Decorated in shades of rose and blue-green with accents of polished brass and sparkling mirrors, Café on the Park is a lovely place to dine.

Owner: The Radisson Hotel
Address: 369 West Vine Street
         Lexington, Kentucky 40507
Telephone: (606) 231-9000
Hours & Days: Monday thru Sunday 6:00 am to 11:00 pm
Reservations not required
MasterCard, Visa, American Express, Discover, Carte Blanche
Directions: On the corner of Vine and Broadway in the heart
             of downtown Lexington. Located on the first level,
             main lobby of the Radisson Plaza Hotel.

BREAKFAST

Starters

Fresh Squeezed Orange or Grapefruit Juice $1.95
Tomato, V8, Prune or Cranberry Juice $1.50
Sectioned Grapefruit $2.50
1/2 Seasonal Melon $2.25
Seasonal Berries $2.25
With cream
Fresh Fruit Medley $3.25
Assorted Yogurts $2.75

Pastries and Such

All are served with butter, preserves and jelly
Muffins or English Muffin $1.50
Croissants $1.95
Toasted Bagel with Cream Cheese $2.25
Toast $1.25
Danish Pastry $1.95
Biscuit and Honey $2.25
Cafe Continental $4.25
Includes juice, breakfast pastry, coffee, decaf, tea or milk

Cafe Specialties

The Breakfast Pizza $6.25
Pizza like shell, filled with ham, sausage, scrambled eggs and melted Monterey Jack cheese
Eggs Derby $5.95
Scrambled eggs with ham and a tomato slice, topped with cheese sauce
The Kentuckian $6.95
Two eggs any style with country ham, biscuits and gravy
Eggs Benedict $6.50
Poached eggs and Canadian bacon on a toasted English muffin topped with hollandaise sauce
Belgian Waffle
With syrup $4.95
With fruit or nuts $5.50
Buttermilk Pancakes
Plain $2.25
With blueberries, pecans or strawberries $2.95
French Toast $3.95
Thick sliced toast, dipped in egg and French toasted and served with warm syrup and butter

Eggs and Omelettes

All of our egg and omelette dishes are served with seasonal fruit garnish, buttered toast or biscuits, jams and preserves, breakfast potatoes or grits
Cheese Omelette $4.95
Three egg omelette with a mixture of cheddar and Monterey jack cheeses
Farmers Omelette $5.25
Three egg omelette with a blend of onion, mushroom, sausage and cheese
Ham and Cheese Omelette $5.50
Three egg omelette with diced ham and cheddar cheese
Two Eggs Any Style $5.50
Choice of bacon, sausage or ham
One Egg Any Style $4.75
Choice of bacon, sausage or ham

Cereals

Oatmeal $2.25
Hot Grits $1.75
Optional with melted cheddar cheese
Assorted Dry Cereals $2.25
Cornflakes, Rice Krispies, Special K, Granola, Raisin Bran, All Bran, Frosted Flakes
With Fruit $.75 Extra

On The Side

Ham $2.50
Canadian Bacon $2.50
Pork Sausage Link or Patty $2.50
Bacon $2.50
Home Fried Potatoes $1.75
Kentucky Country Ham $3.25

Beverages

Coffee $1.00
Decaf Coffee $1.00
Tea $1.00
Hot Chocolate $1.00
Milk $1.00

Café on the Park

LUNCH

Appetizers and Soups

Soup Du Jour $1.95

Beer Cheese Soup $2.25

Chicken Fingers $3.95
With BBQ sauce and honey-mustard sauce

Shrimp $3.95
Pieces of shrimp in cocktail sauce with a lemon wedge

Grouper Fingers $3.95
A mild whitefish, lightly floured, deep fried, and served with mustard sauce

Salads

Cafe Salad $2.50
Mixture of three lettuces, tomatoes, bacon and homemade croutons. Choice of dressing

Sea-Zar Salad $5.75
Romaine lettuce, croutons, fried shrimp and Ceasars dressing

Chicken Salad $5.95
A traditional favorite, served with fresh fruit

Fresh Fruit Plate $5.50
An array of fresh fruit, served with sherbet or cottage cheese and banana nut bread

Vero Beach Cobb Salad $5.75
Shredded lettuce served with turkey, bleu cheese, avocado, bacon, tomato, and black olives in a tortilla shell with dijon vinegrette dressing

Sandwiches

All hot sandwiches include fries

Plaza Club $5.50
A club at its best! With turkey breast, ham, bacon, lettuce, tomato, cheese and chips

Tuna Salad or Chicken Salad Sandwich $4.95
Your choice of tuna or chicken salad served on a French roll with chips

Charbroiled Chicken Sandwich $5.95
Marinated and charbroiled and served on French bread

Reuben $5.50
Thinly sliced corned beef with sauerkraut, Swiss cheese, and thousand island on rye

Steak Sandwich $7.95
Ribeye steak with sauteed mushrooms, green peppers, onions, topped with Monterey jack cheese

Shrimp Sandwich $5.95
Fried shrimp, lettuce, tomato slices on French bread served with tartar sauce

All American Burger $5.75
Charbroiled and served with the works. Your choice of: mushrooms, cheddar, provolone, Swiss, American and bacon

Corbin Fish Sandwich $5.75
Whitefish lightly breaded, with lettuce, tomato and tartar sauce on French bread

Cafe Specialties

Kentucky Hot Brown $5.95
A Kentucky tradition with turkey, ham, mornay sauce, cheddar cheese, bacon and tomato

Mexican Pizza $5.95
Light flour tortilla, topped with pico de gallo, seasoned beef, tomatoes, black olives, green and red peppers, onions, mushrooms and cheese

Stir Fried Chicken and Shrimp $7.25
With peapods, red and yellow peppers and Chinese mushrooms over rice

Fish-N-Chips $6.95
Beer battered with fries and onion straws

Soup and Sandwich $4.95
Ask your server

Omelette du Jour $5.25
Ask your server

Linguine $6.25
Served with your choice of shrimp in a homemade tomato sauce or clams in a basil cream sauce

Beverages

Freshly Brewed Coffee $1.00

Select Herbal or Regular Teas $1.00

Milk $1.00

Perrier $1.00

Soft Drinks $1.00
Coke, Diet Coke, Sprite, Diet Sprite

Imported Beers $2.75

Winners Circle

Kentucky Sky High Pie $2.75
Chocolate, coffee and chocolate ice cream with a bourbon meringue topping

Lexington Lust Pie $2.95
A moist chocolate pecan pie. A favorite in the Kentucky tradition

Chocolate Glob $3.25
Chocolate fudge brownie topped with hot fudge, ice cream, more fudge, whipped cream, nuts and a cherry

Hagen-Daaz Assorted Ice Cream $2.25

Cheesecake with Topping $2.95
Ask your server

DINNER

Appetizers and Soups

Soup Du Jour $1.75

Beer Cheese Soup $2.25

Grouper Fingers $3.95
A mild whitefish, lightly floured, deep fried, and served with mustard sauce

Stuffed Mushroom Caps $5.75
With crabmeat and topped with hollandaise sauce

Escargot $5.95
A favorite served with chef's garlic butter and topped with a delicate pastry

Shrimp Cocktail $6.25
With lemon wedge and cocktail sauce

Hot and Sweet Shrimp $6.95
Jumbo shrimp with a hot sweet sauce served with caramelized garlic

Salads

Cafe Salad $2.50
Mixture of three lettuces, tomatoes, bacon and homemade croutons. Choice of dressing

Sea-Zar Salad $5.75
Romaine lettuce, croutons, fried shrimp and Ceasars dressing

Vero Beach Cobb Salad $5.75
Shredded lettuce served with turkey, bleu cheese, avocado, bacon, tomato, and black olives in a tortilla shell with dijon vinegrette dressing

Sandwiches

Plaza Club $5.50
A club at its best! With turkey breast, ham, bacon, lettuce, tomato, cheese and chips

Kentucky Hot Brown $5.95
A Kentucky tradition with turkey, ham, mornay sauce, cheddar cheese, bacon and tomato

All American Burger $5.75
Charbroiled and served with the works. Your choice of: mushrooms, cheddar, provolone, Swiss, American and bacon

Stylishly Light

Linguine $8.95
Linguine pasta with shrimp and lobster in a basil garlic cream sauce

Grilled Breast of Chicken $8.95
With brandied apples

Chicken Somerset $9.95
Sauteed breast of chicken, with a dijon mustard sauce, artichoke hearts, and mushrooms

San Francisco Chicken and Shrimp $9.95
With peapods, red and yellow peppers, Chinese mushrooms over rice

Cafe Specialties

Avocado Dill Crabcakes $10.95
Fresh dill, avocado, and crabmeat sauteed and served with dill mayo

Walleye Pike $11.95
A local favorite lightly breaded, sauteed, and served with tartar sauce

Grilled Fresh Swordfish $13.50
Served with tomato basil sauce

Shrimp
Done one of the following ways:
  Stuffed with Crab Meat $14.50
  Scampi Style $13.95

Veal Piccata $15.95
Veal medallions sauteed with white wine, a dash of lemon juice, and capers

Veal Lexington $15.95
Milk fed veal with wild mushrooms and madeira flavored demi-glaze

Ribeye Steak $13.95
A hearty cut of choice beef

Filet Mignon $13.95
With bernaise sauce and sauteed mushrooms

Chopped Sirloin Steak $8.95
A Kentucky specialty served with mushrooms and French fries

All of our entrees are served with our Cafe salad, choice of dressing, potato or rice and vegetable, rolls, jalapeno cornbread and butter

Beverages

Freshly Brewed Coffee $1.00

Select Herbal or Regular Teas $1.00

Milk $1.00

Perrier $1.00

Soft Drinks $1.00
Coke, Diet Coke, Sprite, Diet Sprite

Imported Beers $2.75

Winners Circle

Kentucky Sky High Pie $2.75
Chocolate, coffee and chocolate ice cream with a bourbon meringue topping

Lexington Lust Pie $2.95
A moist chocolate pecan pie. A favorite in the Kentucky tradition

Chocolate Glob $3.25
Chocolate fudge brownie topped with hot fudge, ice cream, more fudge, whipped cream, nuts and a cherry

Hagen-Daaz Assorted Ice Cream $2.25

Cheesecake with Topping $2.95
Ask your server

Appetizer

Hot and Sweet Shrimp

6 ounces honey	12 pieces garlic, peeled
1 ounce rice vinegar	Milk to cover
2 teaspoons red peppers, cracked	3 ounces butter
1 teaspoon dry mustard	12 shrimp

Put honey, vinegar, peppers, and dry mustard in a small saucepan and heat. Add more pepper if desired. Peel garlic, place in a small pot, cover with milk, and bring just to a boil. Drain and reserve garlic, discarding milk.

Melt butter in a sauté pan. Add shrimp and garlic, sauté until almost done. Drain butter, add sauce, and finish cooking. Serve 3 shrimp and 3 pieces of garlic per person. Serves 4.

Soup

Beer Cheese Soup

1/2 gallon milk	2 pieces bacon, chopped
1 teaspoon Tabasco sauce	1/4 cup onion, diced
1/2 ounce Worcestershire sauce	16 ounces beer
2 1/2 ounces chicken base	2 1/2 ounces cornstarch
1 8-ounce jar cheese spread	

Bring milk, Tabasco, Worcestershire sauce and chicken base to a boil. While milk mixture is heating, sauté bacon and onion in another pan. Add to milk mixture. Mix cornstarch and beer; add to milk. Add cheese spread and stir with a wire whisk, being careful not to scorch. Makes 1 gallon.

Salad

Vero Beach Cobb Salad

1 floured tortilla	2 ounces medium tomatoes, diced
1/4 head iceberg lettuce, shredded	1 slice cooked bacon, chopped
2 ounces turkey, chopped	1 ounce bleu cheese, crumbled
1 ounce green onions, sliced	1/4 sliced avocado
1 ounce black olives, sliced	Dijon Vinaigrette (see recipe)

Fry tortilla shell in a deep fryer or large pot with hot oil. Hold submerged with a large utensil or can and shape as you desire until crisp, being careful not to burn yourself. (You can buy utensils designed especially for this.) Add all other ingredients as listed and top with 3 to 4 ounces of Dijon vinaigrette. Serves 1.

Dijon Vinaigrette Dressing

2 cups mayonnaise
1/4 cup Dijon mustard
2 ounces vinegar
1 ounce honey

3 tablespoons chopped parsley
1 tablespoon black pepper,
  cracked

Mix all ingredients together and adjust seasonings. Serve chilled. Makes 1 quart.

Chicken Somerset

1 ounce clarified butter
2 to 2 1/2 ounces boneless
  chicken breasts, skinned
3 shiitake mushrooms
4 artichoke hearts, quartered

2 tablespoons Dijon mustard
2 ounces brown sauce*
2 ounces white wine
Chopped parsley

Heat butter in sauté pan. Add chicken and brown on both sides. Remove chicken from pan and add mushrooms, artichoke hearts, mustard, brown sauce and wine. Mix together well. Return chicken to sauce and cook until done. Place chicken on a plate, pour sauce over and sprinkle with chopped parsley. Serves 1.

Quick Brown Sauce:
1/2 clove garlic
2 tablespoons butter
2 tablespoons flour

1 cup canned bouillon
  (or 1 or 2 bouillon cubes dissolved in 1 cup boiling water)

Rub pan with garlic. Melt butter and add flour, stirring until blended. Stir in bouillon and cook to boiling.

Grilled Swordfish
With a Tomato Basil Medley

4 ounces olive oil
3 or 4 tomatoes,
  seeded and chunked
1/4 cup fresh basil, chopped

1 teaspoon chopped garlic
Salt and pepper to taste
4 10-ounce swordfish steaks
2 ounces olive oil

Heat olive oil. Add tomatoes, basil, garlic, salt and pepper and sauté quickly. Remove from pan and set aside.

Brush olive oil on swordfish and cook on a charcoal grill, marking both sides. Cook until done and spoon tomato medley on top. Serves 4.

Entrée

Shrimp and Lobster Linguine

5 ounces clarified butter
1 pound shrimp, cleaned,
  deveined and chopped
  in large chunks
1 pound lobster meat chunks

1/4 cup fresh basil, chopped
1 pint heavy cream
12 ounces linguine, cooked
Salt and pepper to taste
4 fresh basil leaves

Place butter in large sauté pan. Add shrimp and lobster and sauté until half done. Add basil, garlic, and cream. Reduce sauce to 1/2. Add cooked linguini and stir until hot and coated. Divide among four plates and garnish with fresh basil leaves. Serves 4.

Dessert

Sky High Pie

1 pound Oreo cookies, crushed
4 to 6 ounces melted butter
1 quart chocolate ice cream,
  softened

1 quart coffee ice cream, softened
2 ounces Maker's Mark whiskey
6 egg whites
1 pound sugar

Place crushed oreo cookies in a mixing bowl and add melted butter. Mix well, reserving 1/2 cup of crumb mixture. In a springform pan, line bottom and sides with remaining cookie mix, pushing down and packing well.

Beat egg whites until stiff. Slowly add sugar and beat. Set aside.

Layer springform pan with chocolate ice cream, reserved crumb mixture and coffee ice cream. Drizzle whiskey over top. Spoon meringue over ice cream. Place under broiler quickly to add color. Freeze.
Serves 6 to 8.

Casa Galvan

Casa Galvan is a happy family affair for the Galvans and their five daughters, Sheryl, Maria, Toni, Lupe, and Juanita. Mr. And Mrs. Jose Galvan take great pleasure in seeing their family work side by side, and with two Mexican Restaurant locations in Lexington, they all stay quite busy.

Casa Galvan is a place where hearty Mexican food (from their own family recipes) is cooked, home-style, and comes to the table in heaping helpings. Jose Galvan is from Jalico, Mexico, and says Casa Galvan's recipes are definitely influenced by that particular region.

Complimentary salsa and chips arrive while you scan the menu and decide between Enchiladas, Burritos, Tamales, Taquitos, Chili Rellenos, Mexican Shrimp...you get the idea. The food is so good and the prices so right, that you wonder why you ever settled for a plain old burger!

Both locations are informal and dress is strictly casual. On the walls at the downtown spot, portraits of the family share space with Mexican pictures, objects, and memorabilia. The Nicholasville Road restaurant has a more open, airy, and modern feel, and the same south of the border menu.

At noon, on weekdays, the downtown Casa Galvan offers a Mexican buffet. This is a unique opportunity to try a variety of Mexican dishes. Dessert may be a moot point after all this, yet some things are worth the effort! If you save a little room, we can heartily recommend the Creamy Flan. It is a slice of heaven and a heavenly way to end a Mexican meal.

Owners: Las Hermanas Galvan
Address: 149 North Limestone
           Lexington, Kentucky 40503
Telephone: (606) 255-5858
Hours & Days: Monday-Thursday 11:00 am to 9:00 pm
                Friday 11:00 am to 2:00 pm
                Closed Saturday and Sunday
Directions: Downtown on North Limestone.

Address: 1915 Nicholasville Road
           Lexington, Kentucky 40503
Telephone: (606) 278-8977
Hours & Days: Monday-Thursday 11:00 am to 10:00 pm
                Friday-Saturday 11:00 am to 11:00 pm
                Sunday 5:00 pm to 9:00 pm
Reservations not required
Visa, MasterCard, American Express
Directions: Town side of Southland Drive on Nicholasville Road.

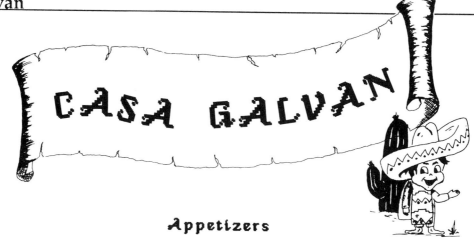

Appetizers

Guacamole................$2.95
Fresh avocados. tomatoes, and
our own spices. Served with
crisp tortilla chips.

Quesadilla................$3.25
2 kinds of cheeses & mild salsa.
Melted between 2 flour tortillas
and topped with your choice of
guacamole or sour cream.

Lupita....................$2.50
Crisp flour tortilla smothered
with cheese and our special salsa.

Nachos......................$2.25
Crisp tortilla chips with lots of
melted cheese, and mild salsa.

Nachos Supreme.........$4.25
Crisp tortilla chips with melted
cheeses, ground beef, Jalapenos,
diced tomatoes, and
sliced black olives.

A LA CARTE

Taco......................$1.30
Enchilada...............$1.30
Tamale $1.50
Taquitos................$2.25
Chile Relleno........... $1.65
Burrito.................. $2.25
Burrito(all Meat)...... $2.65
Special Burrito.........$3.45
Sour Cream..............$.35
Jalapenos.................$.50
Tortillas (2) ....$.50
Guacamole..............$2.95
Small Guacamole......$1.50
Rice or Beans..........$1.10

Soups and Salads

Caldo de Pollo............Bowl $2.25
Chicken soup with vegetables.

Albondigas...Bowl $2.25...Cup $1.25
Mexican soup with meatballs, vegetables and spices.

Tostada.......................$3.75
Crisp corn tortilla layered with beef,
chicken or pork; Refried beans lettuce,
cheese, mild salsa, guacamole, and
sour cream.

Tostada without meat......$3.15

Garden Salad...............$1.30
Fresh mixed salad greens

Dinners
(All dinners served with Rice and Beans)

#1 Taco Dinner	$3.25	#7 Tamale & Enchilada	$4.35
(with 2 Tacos)	$4.25	#8 Tamale, Enchilada & Taco	$5.65
#2 Enchilada Dinner	$3.25	#9 Chile Relleno & Enchilada	$4.50
(With 2 Enchiladas)	$4.25	#10 No.9 & Taquito	$5.90
#3 Taquito Dinner	$3.60	#11 Burrito Dinner	$3.60
(includes 2 Taquitos)		(with 2 Burritos)	$4.95
#4 Enchilada & Taco	$4.25	#12 Enchilada & Taquitos	$4.90
#5 Burrito & Taco	$4.90	#13 Burrito & Taquitos	$5.55
#6 Burrito & Enchilada	$4.90	#14 Tamale & Taco	4.35

#15 Enchilada, Burrito, & Taquito $6.30

Special Plates

Carnita's Dinner...$4.95
Tender pieces of seasoned, deep fried pork. Served with guacamole, rice, refried beans, and tortillas.

Steak Picado...$6.50
Tender beef tips simmered in a special sauce with tomatoes, onion, and bell pepper. Served with rice, refried beans, and tortillas.

Carne Asada..$6.50
Grilled 8 Oz. Tenderloin, rice refried beans, and tortillas.

Mexican Shrimp..$ 6.50
Butterfly shrimp sauteed in butter with onions, bell peppers, and tomatoes. Served with rice, refried beans and tortillas.

Drinks

Soft Drinks..$.70
(Pepsi, Mountain Dew, Dr. Pepper, Diet Pepsi Free, Or 7Up)
Coffee...$.50
(Bottomless Cup)
Tea...$.60
(Bottomless Glass)
Milk...................................Small $.35.....Large $.70

Dessert

Flan..$1.75
Kahlua Moose..$1.50

CATERING SERVICES AVAILABLE - ASK YOUR WAITRESS FOR DETAILS.

Nachos Supreme

Medium size bowl of
  nacho chips
2 cups cheddar cheese
1/2 cup mild picante sauce
1 tomato, diced

2 jalapeño peppers, diced
1/4 cup black olives, chopped
Ground beef or chicken,
  optional

In an oven proof bowl, place half of nacho chips on bottom. Cover with half of cheese, another layer of chips, and top with remaining cheese. Bake at 350 degrees for 3 to 5 minutes or until cheese is melted. Remove from oven and top with picante sauce, tomato, jalapeños, and olives. If using meat, place cooked meat between first and second layer of chips. Serves 4.

Caldo De Pollo
(Chicken Soup)

1 whole chicken, separated
5 potatoes, diced
4 carrots, diced
2 stalks celery, diced
1 onion, quartered

1/2 tablespoon salt
1/4 teaspoon pepper
1/4 teaspoon garlic powder
1 lemon, sliced

Boil chicken 30 minutes. Add vegetables and spices, and cook an additional 40 to 50 minutes, or until meat falls from bone. Serve hot with lemon slices. Serves 5.

Mexican Shrimp

30 to 40 medium-size shrimp,
  peeled and deveined
1 tomato
1 bell pepper
1 onion
4 cups cooked pinto beans, warm

1/2 cup grated cheddar cheese
Salt and pepper to taste
1/2 stick butter
4 cups cooked rice, warm
1 package flour tortillas

Butterfly shrimp. Cut tomato, pepper, and onion into bite size pieces. Mash pinto beans in saucepan or skillet; top with cheddar cheese. Season shrimp to taste, and sauté in butter 3 minutes. Add vegetables and stir 3 to 4 minutes. Serve with heated rice and beans. For soft tacos, heat tortillas on grill. Serves 4.

Quesadilla
(Mexican Pizza)

1 package flour tortillas
4 cups grated cheeses,
  any combination

1/2 pint picante sauce,
  hot or mild
1 small carton sour cream

Heat grill to 350 degrees. Place one tortilla on grill, cover with cheeses and sauce; top with another tortilla. Grill 60 seconds, turn and grill an additional 30 seconds. Place on round plates and cut into 6 to 8 slices. Top with sour cream. Makes 6 quesadillas.

Dessert

Gabilanes

1 package flour tortillas
4 cups sugar and
  cinnamon mixture
  (color should be light brown)

Cut tortillas into 8 pie shapes and separate. Heat deep fryer to 350 degrees and place small portions of tortillas in oil, stirring gently, for approximately 2 minutes. Remove from oil, place hot tortillas in sugar and cinnamon mixture, and toss. Place in a bowl and serve. Serves 20.

Dessert

Mansanitas

1 package flour tortillas   **Sugar**
6 fresh apples or 2 cans apples,   **Cinnamon**
  chopped   **Ice Cream**

Lay each tortilla on a flat surface and place 2 tablespoons of apples on one end. Roll tortilla and toothpick tortillas in pairs. Place in deep fryer for approximately 3 minutes. Remove, and immediately roll tortillas in a sugar and cinnamon mixture. Remove toothpicks and top with ice cream. Serves 6.

C'est Si Bon!

Louis Cease, one of the trailblazers of fine gourmet dining in Lexington, has opened a charming new restaurant called C'est Si Bon! Offering French and Continental cuisine, C'est Si Bon! has developed an impressive following of savvy diners after just one year.

Chef Cease is pictured in his element in a wonderful portrait beside the front door. It perfectly captures his quiet, but intense dedication to culinary excellence. His fifteen years in Paris first piqued an interest in gourmet cooking and prompted his study at the prestigious La Varrene. Working with Julia Child and James Beard, he was encouraged to pursue and receive La Grande Diplome and to become a Certified Executive Chef. In 1986, he was named a Travel Holiday Magazine Award Winning Chef for his efforts with his 4-star restaurant, Bistro.

C'est Si Bon! is decorated with cool, dark, floral wallpaper, soft green carpet, fresh sprays of gladioluses, and prints by Impressionists Tissot, Renoir, Monet, and Degas. Tuesday through Saturday night a harpist plays in the dining room.

Veal C'est Si Bon! is a popular entrée with regulars, as are the Veal Sweetbreads (an unusual and delicious offering) and the fresh seafood. All soufflés are prepared from scratch, and you may choose from either vegetable or dessert. You may prefer to end your meal with Chocolate Decadence (a dessert that speaks for itself)!

Louis and Sharon Cease have put their warmth and welcome and considerable wisdom into this fine restaurant, and it shows.

Owners: Louis and Sharon Cease
Address: 735 East Main Street
          Lexington, Kentucky 40502
Telephone: (606) 269-3269
Hours & Days: Lunch: Monday-Friday 11:00 am to 2:00 pm
               Dinner: Monday-Thursday 6:00 pm to 10:00 pm
                        Friday-Saturday 6:00 pm to 11:00 pm
Reservations recommended
All major credit cards accepted
Directions: Corner of East Main Street and Ashland Avenue.

Louis Cease's

French and Continental Cuisine

C'est Si Bon!

Delightful Beginnings

Escargot Bourguignonne
French Snails baked in Garlic, Parsley, Shallots, and Lemon Butter ... $6.00

With Brie $7.50

Smoked Scottish Salmon
Prepared with Onions, Capers and Olive Oil and served with Toast Points $7.00

Gravlax
Marinated Salmon served with a sweet Mustard Sauce and Toast Points ... $7.00

Coquilles St. Jacque A La Provencale
Sea Scallops prepared with Wine, Garlic and Herbs $7.00

Shrimp Chef's Style
Six large Shrimp prepared with Amaretto, Brandy and Cream $7.00

Tortellini Pasta
Prepared with Italian Sun-Dried Tomatoes, Mushrooms, Romano Cheese and smothered in a rich Cream Sauce........ $5.50

With shrimp $7.00

Classic Spicy-Stuffed Mushrooms
Stuffed with Snowcrab and Gruyere Cheese, served on a Bed of Lettuce $6.75

Silver-Tip Mussels
Seven Mussels steamed in Saffron, Thyme and White Wine $7.00

Crab en Croute
Crab Meat in Puff Pastry with Gruyere Cheese $6.00

Carpaccio
Thin medallions of raw Beef on a plate glazed with Olive Oil and garnished with Anchovy fillets, roasted Green Peppers and Capers and served with a Mustard Sauce........ $6.95

French Onion Soup
Served with lots of Romano Cheese and Croutons $3.00

Soup Du Jour
Chef's Special Daily Creation $3.50

Seafood Bisque $4.00

Pate's
Lasagnes aux L'egumes
Vegetable Lasagna Pâté' $4.50

As Entree $13.95

Gooseliver Pate'
Gooseliver Pâté' prepared with Truffles in a Puff Pastry and topped with a Mustard Cucumber Sauce $6.95

Beluga Caviar
A one-ounce serving garnished with cooked Egg Yolk and Egg White, Onion, Parsley and Sour Cream and served with Toast Points $55.00

Salads

House Salad
Our House Salad served with your choice of Ranch, Bleu Cheese, Honey Mustard, Thousand Island, French or our house dressing of Vinaigrette

$3.75

Caesar For One
Romaine lettuce with a blend of Anchovies, Eggs, Parmesan Cheese and Croutons

$4.00

$7.50 For Two

Salad Extravaganza
Don't Miss Our Unique Daily Creations

$4.50

Main

Our main courses are served with your choice of Potatoes or Rice. Also included is our House Salad, Vegetables of the Day and French Bread.

Henri IV $17.75
A center-cut Filet of Tenderloin Mesquite-grilled to your temperature and served with your choice of Bernaise, Choron, Garlic or Diane Sauces.

Duke of Wellington $17.85
Beef Tenderloin prepared medium rare to medium temperature, topped with pâté and wrapped and baked in a Puff Pastry. Served with Hunter Sauce.

Seafood Wellington $18.50
Fresh fish pâté made from Fish du jour, wrapped and baked in pastry and topped with Shrimp Sauce.

Fish Du Jour .... Priced Daily
Several choices of the freshest Fish prepared to perfection. Your choice of Baked, Grilled, Poached or Steamed in Parchment Paper.

Lamb Cutlets Villandry $17.00
Tender Lamb Cutlets flavored with Tarragon and their juices deglazed with Vouvray. Served with Artichoke bases filled with Duxell of Mushroom.

Tournedos Rossini $18.00
Beef Tenderloin Fillet grilled to your temperature. Topped with Foie gras and served with Espagnole Sauce.

Medallions De Veau Alexandra $17.75
Provimi Veal Medallions sauteed with soybean oil, their juices deglazed with Maderia Wine and Marsala Sherry and garnished with five varieties of Imported Mushrooms: Shiitake, Oyster, Lobster, Morels and Chinese.

Veau Scallops in Lemon Sauce $16.00
White Veal Escallops sauteed in White Wine with Shallots and fresh Lemon.

C'est Si Bon! Our House Speciality $17.98
*White Provimi Veal prepared with Borsin Cheese filling and a Lemon Zest Breading.
It's so Good!*

Ris De Veau $13.90
*Veal Sweetbreads sauteed in Cream, deglazed with Vermouth, Maderia and Brandy
and served with a light French Mustard Sauce.*

Tournedos Au Poivre A La Crème $18.00
*Beef Tenderloin filet coated with a Pepper Sauce of Wine, Cream, Tomato, Brandy and
Red and Green Peppercorns. Creates a special flavor - strong but fresh!*

Chicken Oscar $15.00
*A boneless, skinless Breast of Chicken, sauteed in Vegetable Oil and topped with Snow
Crab Meat and Hollandaise Sauce.*

Three-In-One $13.00
*A boneless, skinless Breast of Chicken stuffed with three Imported Cheeses and served
with a Zesty Lemon Sauce.*

Chicken in White Wine $12.00
*A boneless, skinless Breast of Chicken sauteed in Chardonnay with Domestic
Mushrooms.*

Coquilles St. Jaque $14.25
*Fresh Scallops prepared with Garlic, Parsley, and White Wine, or the Classic, prepared
with Tomatoes, Mushrooms and Cream.*

Breast of Duck $14.95
*Boneless Mesquite-grilled Breast of Duck prepared with Apple Butter, Red Wine and
a Black Walnut Sauce.*

Prime Rib $13.50
*A Lipon Ribeye prepared to your temperature and served with cracked Black Pepper-
corns and Grand Marnier Sauce.*

Calve's Liver $10.00
Provimi Veal Liver sauteed with Onions and a Demi Glace Sauce.

Chef's Daily Creations . . . . *Priced Daily*
Scrumptious specials created and prepared daily by Chef Cease.

*Note From the Chef: Chef Cease uses soybean or vegetable oils for sauteeing and
Clarified Butter and Olive Oils for his sauces. For seasoning, he uses Sea Salt or Rock
Salt, Peppercorns, Fresh Herbs and Juices and Wines.*

Desserts $4.00
Made fresh daily and waiting to tempt your palate.

*If a dish is missing from our menu, do not be disappointed. Chef Cease chooses only the best market selections
and will not use those of less quality.*

Louis J. Cease
Certified Executive Chef
Travel/Holiday Magazine
Award-winning Chef

Black Bean Soup

2 cups dried black beans
Salt
2 to 4 cups canned chicken stock
Olive oil
1 cup onions, chopped
3 teaspoons garlic,
  finely chopped
8 ounces lean ham,
  cooked and chopped

1 large tomato, peeled,
  chopped, and seeded
2 tablespoons malt vinegar
1/2 teaspoon cumin
Cracked black pepper
Sour cream

Wash beans in a colander under cold running water until the draining water is clear. Transfer to a heavy 3 to 4 quart casserole and add 1 tablespoon salt. Cover the beans with water by at least 2 inches. Bring to boil and simmer 2 hours or until tender enough to mash beans against sides of pan with spoon. Add chicken stock to the beans to equal 6 cups of liquid. Cool and blend 1 cup of beans and 1 cup of liquid in blender. Blend.

In 5 quart casserole, heat oil, and add onions and garlic. Stir until transparent. Add ham, tomato, vinegar, cumin, and a small amount of black pepper. Bring to a boil and cook to coating consistency. Add bean mixture, simmer over low heat until well heated. Serve at once. Serves 6.

Shrimp, Corn and Potato Soup

1 pound medium shrimp,
  peeled and deveined
2 tablespoons butter
1 cup onions, finely chopped
1 teaspoon garlic, finely chopped
3 large ripe tomatoes,
  peeled, seeded, and chopped
  or 1 1/2 cups canned tomatoes
1 cup fish stock, clam juice,
  or water

2 whole cloves
1 small bay leaf
2 teaspoons salt
Black pepper, freshly ground
6 new potatoes
2 cups milk
1 cup heavy cream
2 ears corn, shucked and cut

Cut shrimp crosswise into 1/2 inch pieces and set aside. In 2 to 3 quart saucepan, melt butter over moderate heat. When foam subsides, add onions and garlic and cook 5 minutes, or until they are soft and transparent, but not brown. Add tomatoes, stock, cloves, bay leaf, salt, and pepper and bring to a boil. Reduce heat to low, cover, and simmer 15 minutes.

Pour entire contents of saucepan into foodmill or food processor and purée. Return to saucepan. Peel potatoes and cut into ovals 2 inches long and 1 inch thick; add to ingredients in saucepan and bring to a boil. Reduce heat, cover, and simmer for 30 minutes. Do not let potatoes fall apart. Stir in milk, cream, and corn. Cover and simmer 5 minutes. Drop in shrimp and cook, covered, 4 to 5 minutes or until shrimp turns pink. Correct seasonings. Serves 4 to 6.

Breaded Veal Scallops with Brown Butter

6 veal scallops, 1/4 pound each
Salt
Red peppercorns or paprika
1 egg
6 teaspoons vegetable oil

1/4 pound stale French bread,
  grated to crumbs
8 to 9 tablespoons
  unsalted butter
Juice of 1/2 lemon

Flatten scallops with mallet or flat side of a cleaver, breaking fiber of meat and spreading out scallops. The scallops should be thin enough to read a paper through. Season on both sides with salt and pepper. Beat egg in bowl with a pinch of salt and 1/2 teaspoon of oil. Dip scallops in egg mixture, thinly coat with bread crumbs, and press firmly so crumbs will stick. Heat 4 tablespoons butter and 6 teaspoons of oil in large skillet. Season scallops well and brown until bread crumbs are golden, approximately 8 minutes. Place scallops on heated platter. Discard oil and melt 4 tablespoons butter in skillet. Brown butter lightly. Squeeze lemon juice into butter and pour over scallops. Serves 6.

Coq au Vin Sauté à la Louis

1 4-pound broiler hen
Salt and freshly ground pepper
Marinade*
2 cups water
8 tablespoons butter
2/3 cups brandy or burgundy

2 large onions
8 ounces salt pork or bacon,
  blanched and cut in cubes
12 small white onions
1 tablespoon powdered sugar
Fresh mushrooms

Cut chicken into drumsticks, thighs, and halved breasts. Sprinkle with salt and pepper. Combine all ingredients for marinade and marinate for 12 hours. Save wings, neck, and gizzard.

Cook wings, neck, and gizzard for 3 minutes in water. Save broth. Preheat oven to 350 degrees. Drain chicken and strain marinade. Dry chicken with paper towel. Sauté in 1/4 cup butter until brown. Place chicken in baking pan. Flame sauté pan with brandy and add onions with 2 tablespoons butter. When onions are translucent, add marinade, and boil until almost dry. Purée mixture and add reserved broth. Season chicken and cover with sauce. Cover and bake in moderate oven for 30 minutes.

Fry salt pork cubes until crisp. Add onions and sugar and sauté lightly. Repeat with mushrooms. After cooking chicken, skim fat from top and remove chicken. If sauce is thin, tighten with a roux. Add pork, onions and mushrooms. Serve over thin noodles cooked al denté. Serves 4.

*Marinade:
1 bottle red wine
1 onion, chopped
1 carrot, chopped
1 celery stick, chopped

1 bay leaf
Parsley
1 clove of garlic, chopped

Mix together.

Veal Escallops with Yogurt

2 pounds veal shoulder,
  sliced 1/4 inch thick
Salt
Ground black or
  red peppercorns
1/2 stick of butter
3/4 cup sliced onions

20 small mushroom caps
1 tablespoon flour
1/3 cup heavy cream
1/3 cup water
1/2 cup plain yogurt
2 teaspoons paprika

Cut veal into strips 1 inch wide. Flatten with side of cleaver. Sprinkle with salt and pepper. Sauté in heavy skillet in 2 tablespoons butter. Remove veal to warm plate and keep hot. In same skillet, add remaining butter, onions, and mushrooms. Season with salt and pepper. Stir until lightly brown. Transfer to veal dish. Melt remaining butter in skillet, blend in flour and brown lightly. Add cream and water, mix well, and bring to boil, stirring constantly. Remove from heat. Beat yogurt and pour into skillet along with paprika. Heat, but do not boil. Add meat, onions and mushrooms. Correct seasonings. Serve warm with wild rice. Serves 6.

Coach House of Lexington

The Coach House of Lexington has for years been the restaurant Lexingtonians think of when celebrating birthdays or anniversaries...or Fridays...or even Tuesdays! Any excuse to dine at the Coach House is a good one, as every meal is special!

Stanley Demos brought his expertise to The Coach House in June of 1969. Its crystal chandeliers, elegant artwork, fresh flowers, and impeccable service reflected the French tastes he had acquired as maître d'hôtel of Cincinnati's finest restaurant, The Maisonette. The Coach House quickly achieved prominence in the restaurant industry, and by 1973 received the first of its 17 Travel-Holiday Awards as well as the Mobil Four Star Award.

Purchased by his daughter and son-in-law in April of 1988, the restaurant has undergone a complete renovation, while continuing the tradition of spectacular flower arrangements and the highest quality of food preparation.

Now featuring American Regional Cuisine with a Continental flair, the menu includes grilled seafood flown in fresh daily and delicious black Angus sirloin.

Their extensive wine list has received the Award of Distinction of 1989 from the "Winespectator Magazine" and showcases premier California and European vintages.

A great many people remember special moments spent at The Coach House, but why live in the past? It's time to create new memories at a Coach House that is better than ever!

Owners: Samuel P. and Elizabeth Demos Nelson
Address: 855 South Broadway
 Lexington, Kentucky 40504
Telephone: (606) 252-7777
Hours & Days: Lunch: Monday-Friday 11:00 am to 2:30 pm
 Dinner: Monday-Saturday 5:00 pm to 10:30 pm
 Closed on Sunday
Reservations recommended
MasterCard, Visa, American Express, Diner's Club, Carte Blanche
Directions: South on Broadway, approximately 1 mile from
 the center of town.

The Coach House

Appetizers

JUMBO GULF SHRIMP SERVED CHILLED with Two Sauces	7.00
NORWEGIAN SMOKED SALMON with a Mustard-Dill Sauce and Traditional Garnishes	7.00
THE CRABE DEMOS Baked Lump Crabmeat on Wild Rice, Curried-Mayonnaise Sauce	7.50
ESCARGOTS BAKED IN GARLIC BUTTER Crusty French Bread	5.50
SPINACH AND EGG TORTELLINI Tossed in Rich Alfredo Sauce with Green Peas and Mushrooms	6.00
OUR FAMOUS MARYLAND CRABCAKES with an Egg and Dill Mornay	6.50
DEEP-FRIED JACK CHEESE "MONTEREY" with Guacamole and Sour Cream	5.50
BAKED STUFFED SHRIMP with Lump Crabmeat, Smoked Bacon, and a Kentucky Bourbon Barbecue Sauce	7.00

Soups

TODAY'S SOUP CREATIONS	2.00
BAKED ONION SOUP French Bread Croutons, Provolone and Romano Cheeses	3.00
A SAMPLING OF ALL THREE SOUPS	2.50
CHILLED SEASONAL SOUP Special Creation-of-the-Day	2.00

Salads

THE GREEK SALAD Prepared Tableside with Our Oregano-Vinaigrette	2.50
STEAK CUT TOMATOES AND BERMUDA ONIONS on Bibb Lettuce with E.V. Olive Oil, Lemon and Fresh Basil	3.00
KENTUCKY LIMESTONE BIBB Lettuce, Champagne Dressing	2.50
THE CAESAR SALAD Prepared Tableside	3.00
OUR FRESH SPINACH SALAD Creamy Bacon Dressing and Sugared Walnuts	3.00

SAMUEL P. NELSON
ELIZABETH DEMOS NELSON
PROPRIETORS

THE STANLEY DEMOS COOKBOOK	10.00
CHAMPAGNE DRESSING	1.50

Fresh Vegetables

OUR FAMOUS FRENCH-FRIED SWEET POTATOES with Cinnamon Sugar	3.00
FRESH MUSHROOMS SAUTEED in Garlic Butter, White Wine and Lemon	2.50
FRESH EGGPLANT ROMANO in a Light Batter, with Marinara	3.00
FRESH ASPARAGUS, in Season, with Hollandaise or Lemon-Butter	4.00

Seafood Entrees

SOLE MY WAY, One of My Father's Favorites	14.00
CHARBROILED SCAMPI with Garlic Butter for Dipping	20.00
FRESH RED SNAPPER SAUTEED with Pecan Butter	18.00
CHARGRILLED NORWEGIAN SALMON with Chef's Sauce-of-the-Day	18.00
GEORGIA FARM-RAISED CATFISH with Crisped Bacon, Red and Green Peppers in Browned Butter	14.00
OUR FAMOUS MARYLAND CRABCAKES with an Egg and Dill Mornay	15.00
BAKED STUFFED SHRIMP with Lump Crabmeat, Smoked Bacon, and a Kentucky Bourbon Barbecue Sauce	17.00
FRIED SHRIMP with Two Sauces	13.00

Meat Entrees

CHARGRILLED CHICKEN COACH HOUSE with Kentucky Country Ham and Sauce Supreme	15.00
CHICKEN PICCATA in Seasoned Breadcrumbs and Browned Butter	13.00
SAUTEED CHICKEN GRENOBLE with White Wine, Lemon and Capers	13.00
VEAL FRANCAISE, A Coach House Tradition	18.00
VEAL MARSALA with a Robust Wine Sauce	18.00
CALVES' LIVER SAUTEED with Smoked Bacon or Sweet Onions	12.00
BROILED LOIN LAMBCHOPS with Fresh Rosemary Butter	22.00
OUR FAMOUS LAMB RACK in Natural Au Jus, with Traditional Garnishes	20.00
FILET MIGNON DIANE Prepared Tableside	17.00
BLACK ANGUS SIRLOIN STEAK with a Light Garlic Butter	18.00

Your Safety is Important to Us.
We Encourage You to Not Mix Drinking and Driving.
Please Consult the Front Desk to Arrange Transportation.

Crabe Demos

1 cup mayonnaise
4 teaspoons prepared mustard
3 teaspoons curry powder
1/2 teaspoon salt

2 teaspoons lemon juice
1/2 cup wild rice, cooked
6 ounces lump crabmeat
Parmesan cheese

Combine mayonnaise, mustard, curry, salt and lemon juice; set aside. Divide wild rice into two sea shells. Cover with crabmeat. Spread mayonnaise mixture over crabmeat. Sprinkle with grated Parmesan cheese and bake for 20 minutes in hot oven.

Serve each shell as a first course or luncheon dish. Serves 2.

Escargots de Bourgogne

12 ounces butter, softened
1 teaspoon garlic, chopped
1 teaspoon shallots, chopped
1 tablespoon parsley, chopped

1/4 teaspoon salt
1 teaspoon lemon juice
24 snails

Place butter in small bowl; add remaining ingredients, except snails, and mix well. Drain liquid from snails. Place 1/3 teaspoon of garlic mixture in the opening of each snail shell. Insert snail and press so that snail will be completely inside shell. Seal opening with an additional 1/2 teaspoon of garlic butter. Set shells on a snail plate* and bake in a medium oven. When butter foams, take out and garnish with parsley. Serve with wedges of lemon and French or Italian bread. Serves 8.

*Note: If you do not have a snail plate, improvise by placing 1/2 inch of salt in a pie pan. Set opening of snails upright so that when butter melts, it will not run out.

Cheddar Cheese Soup

3 tablespoons onion, grated
3 tablespoons carrots, grated
1/2 stick butter
2 13-ounce cans chicken broth
1/2 teaspooon dry mustard

4 tablespoons cornstarch
1/4 cup milk
1 cup sharp cheddar cheese, grated
Garlic croutons

Sauté onions and carrots in butter for 3 minutes. Add broth and dry mustard; simmer for 5 minutes. Mix cornstarch with milk and pour into boiling broth, beating with a wire whisk. Simmer soup until thickened; add grated cheese and continue to simmer until cheese melts. Top with garlic croutons and serve in cups. Serves 4 to 6.

Gazpacho Coach House

1/2 cup cucumbers
1/2 cup fresh tomatoes, peeled
1/4 cup green peppers
1/4 cup pimientos
1/4 cup onions

1/4 cup celery
3 tablespoons olive oil
1 tablespoon wine vinegar
Salt and pepper to taste
Tomato juice

Finely chop all vegetables and place in a quart jar. Add olive oil, vinegar, salt and pepper. Fill jar with tomato juice. Shake well and refrigerate. Serve very cold. Serves 4 to 6.

Spinach Salad with Warm Bacon Dressing

1/2 cup virgin olive oil
Crushed fresh peppercorns,
    to taste
1/2 cup sliced mushrooms
1/2 cup chopped bacon
1 teaspoon bacon grease
1/3 cup red onions, chopped

1 teaspoon sugar
2 teaspoons Worcestershire sauce
1 teaspoon Dijon mustard
1 tablespoon red wine vinegar
1 1/2 ounces cognac
3/4 cup sour cream
5 cups fresh spinach

Heat olive oil in pan to medium temperature. Add ground pepper, mushrooms, bacon, bacon grease, and onions; sauté for approximately 1 1/2 minutes. Mix sugar, Worcestershire sauce and mustard; add to pan, stirring constantly. Add vinegar and flame with cognac. While pan is still flaming, add sour cream, mixing thoroughly. Adjust pepper if necessary. In a separate bowl, toss spinach with dressing until coated; let rest for 30 seconds. Serves 2.

Chicken with Bing Cherries
for Four

4 8-ounce chicken breasts
Salt and pepper to taste
1 cup flour
1/2 cup vegetable shortening

1 29-ounce (#2 1/2) can
    bing cherries
2 tablespoons cornstarch
2 ounces cherry liqueur

Salt and pepper each breast and roll in flour. Sauté in vegetable shortening on both sides until golden and done. Transfer to large oval platter or individual dinner plate. Place bing cherries in a saucepan and bring to a boil. Dissolve cornstarch in cherry liqueur and add to boiling cherry juice. Simmer until cherries thicken and sauce is transparent. Divide over chicken breasts. Serves 4.

Dover Sole My Way

12 filets of Dover sole
1 cup flour
1/2 cup vegetable shortening
1/3 stick butter
1 medium onion, diced
2 cloves garlic, finely chopped

1 cup tomatoes,
   drained and diced
2 tablespoons parsley,
   chopped
Salt and pepper to taste
l cup Hollandaise Sauce*
Chopped parsley for garnish

Dust filets in flour. Sauté in vegetable shortening until golden in color. When done, arrange in a flat baking dish, placing filets side by side.

For tomato sauce: Melt butter in a heavy skillet. Add onions and cook until transparent. Add garlic and sauté 10 seconds longer. Add tomatoes, parsley and seasoning.

To assemble dish: Using a teaspoon, divide tomato sauce over each filet. Spoon Hollandaise sauce over tomato sauce. Sprinkle with chopped parsley. Place under broiler and cook until sauce is bubbly. Serves 4.

Hollandaise Sauce:
3 egg yolks
2 tablespoons lemon juice

Pinch of cayenne pepper
4 tablespoons butter

In blender, mix egg yolks, lemon juice and cayenne pepper for 3 seconds on high. Melt butter in saucepan until bubbly. With blender on high, slowly add butter to egg mixture in a steady stream. Keep warm until ready to serve.

Strawberries Amandes

2 tablespoons toasted almonds,
   sliced
1 tablespoon butter
1 ounce cognac or brandy
2 cups fresh strawberries, sliced

2 ounces strawberry liqueur
5 1/2 tablespoons
   pure cane sugar, or less to taste
1 1/2 ounces Amaretto liqueur
Vanilla ice cream

Sauté almonds in butter over medium heat until bubbling. Flame with cognac and add 1/2 of strawberries. Mash strawberries in pan until syrupy, allowing small pieces of strawberries to remain. Add strawberry liqueur, increase heat, and reduce liquid. Sprinkle with 2 1/2 tablespoons sugar. Add Amaretto, and reduce again. Stir in 1 tablespoon sugar and remaining strawberries. Add remainder of sugar and cook until heated completely. Serve over vanilla ice cream. Serves 2.

Columbia Steak House

If you happen to be anywhere near Lexington when a serious steak craving strikes, Columbia Steak House is the place you want to remember. There are three convenient locations from which to choose, so your craving can be satisfied quickly and oh, so deliciously.

Voted Lexington's favorite dinner spot in "Your Business Magazine", Columbia has been offering memorable meals for nearly forty years. All the steaks are cut at their own commissary.

The most popular dinner at Columbia has always been the Special, served with a Diego Salad. The Special consists of a juicy tenderloin of beef, broiled in garlic butter, and served with a large, fluffy baked potato or steak fries and bread. The Diego Salad can be ordered for one or two and is a crunchy old-fashioned delight, unencumbered with the latest fad in lettuce or trendy dressings. Plenty of fish, chicken, and sandwiches are served here, too, as well as a Kentucky Hot Brown and lamb fries.

The owner, Courtenay Lancaster, has brought her beautiful touch to the two newest Columbia locations in the red and blue colors of her family farm, Calumet. The racing silks, which have been in the winner's circle for so many horse races, have been lovingly framed behind glass, the silk banners of different horse farms hung from the ceiling, and Calumet's colors have been repeated throughout the dining room in imaginative ways.

The Columbia Steak House reputation has been secured by a very loyal and continually growing clientele over the years. With the combination of consistently good food, and reasonable prices, Columbia will no doubt be around for another forty years or more.

Owner: (Mrs.) Courtenay Lancaster

Address: 201 North Limestone
    Lexington, Kentucky 40507
Telephone: (606) 253-3135
Hours & Days:
  Monday-Thursday 5:00 pm to 11:00 pm
  Friday-Saturday 5:00 pm to 2:00 am
  Closed Sundays
Banquet facilities available
Directions: Downtown Lexington on
    North Limestone.

Address: 1435 Alexandria Drive,
    Lexington, Kentucky 40504
Telephone: (606) 233-4185 or (606) 233-0449
Hours & Days:
  Monday-Thursday 5:00 pm to 11:00 pm
  Friday-Saturday 5:00 pm to 1:00 am
  Closed Sundays
Banquet facilities available
Directions: Versailles Road north
    on Alexandria Drive.

Address: 3347 Tates Creek Pike
    Lexington, Kentucky 40502
Telephone: (606) 268-1666
Hours & Days:
  Monday-Thursday 5:00 pm to 11:00 pm
  Friday-Saturday 5:00 pm to 1:00 am
  Sunday 11:00 am to 10:00 pm
  Lunch: 11:30 am to 5:00 pm daily
    except Saturday
Directions: Tates Creek Road in the
    Lansdowne Shopping Center.

All locations:
Reservations accepted for large parties only
Visa, MasterCard, American Express accepted

Columbia Steak House

APPETIZERS

Chicken Strips	$4.25
Fried Banana Peppers	3.45
Shrimp Cocktail	4.95
Lamb Fry Appetizer	$3.95
Buffalo Chicken Wings	3.95
New Orleans-style Shrimp	5.95

COLUMBIA STEAK HOUSE

SPECIAL

A carefully selected tenderloin of beef broiled to your order in garlic butter, served with baked potato or Columbia's Steak fries, bread and butter $9.95

STEAKS

All steaks are broiled to order. Served with choice of baked potato or Columbia's Steak fries, bread and butter.

Grilled onions and mushrooms ..... $.75

Tenderloin of Beef (Our specialty—broiled and served in garlic butter)	$ 9.95
New York Strip	11.95
T-Bone	11.95
Ribeye	10.95

TRADITIONAL COLUMBIA ENTREES

Served with choice of baked potato or Columbia's Steak fries, bread and butter.

Hot Brown	$5.95
Lamb Fries	7.95

DIEGO SALAD
Columbia's Famous Diego Salad —
try with our house dressing.

Enough for 2	$2.50
Individually	1.50

Columbia's
SAUTEED MUSHROOMS
$1.75

WE REGRET THAT WE CANNOT ACCEPT CHECKS

FAVORITES

Served with your choice of any one of our daily vegetables and baked potato
or Columbia's Steak fries, bread and butter.

Prime Rib: Regular $10.95
             Large 12.95

Rotisserie Roasted Half Chicken 8.45
Chicken Monterey 8.95

SEAFOOD

Served with your choice of any one of our daily vegetables and baked potato
or Columbia's Steak fries, bread and butter.

Broiled Halibut .... $ 9.95
Fried Shrimp 10.45
Wall-Eye Pike (served fried) 9.95
Broiled Orange Roughy 9.95

SANDWICHES

Hamburger $3.25
    Add any of these toppings for .35 each: American, Swiss, cheddar cheeses,
    grilled onions, mushrooms, bacon
French Dip with Swiss 4.95
Fish Sandwich 4.95
Club 4.95

SALADS

Diego Salad $2.50
Individual Diego Salad 1.50
Head Lettuce w/choice of dressing .. 1.95
Sliced Tomato with onion 1.75
Soup of the day .... (cup) 1.25

BEVERAGES

Soft Drinks .... $.85
Milk .... .85
Coffee .... .85
Tea .... .85

SIDE ORDERS
Columbia's Steak Fries $1.50
Fresh Vegetable .... .95
Baked Potato 1.95
Baked Potato with cheese 2.45
Baked Potato w/cheese & bacon 2.95

CARRY-OUT SERVICE
AVAILABLE

253-3135   233-4185   268-1666
Limestone Alexandria Tates Creek

 WE PROUDLY SERVE PEPSI PRODUCTS

New Orleans Style BBQ Shrimp

6 tablespoons unsalted butter
1 1/2 teaspoons ground
  black pepper
1 1/2 teaspoons cracked
  black pepper
1 teaspoon Creole seasoning*
3 tablespoons
  Worcestershire sauce

1 teaspoon chopped garlic
1 tablespoon lemon juice
1/2 teaspoon whole rosemary
18 pieces shrimp (41 to 50 count),
  peeled, deveined, with tails on
Garlic toast

Melt butter in sauté pan over medium heat. Add remaining ingredients, except shrimp and toast; simmer for 2 minutes. Stir in shrimp and sauté an additional 1 1/2 minutes. Pour entire mixture into a bowl. Garnish with garlic toast for dipping. Serves 1 to 2.

Creole Seasoning:
4 tablespoons salt
1 1/2 tablespoons garlic salt
3 tablespoons ground
  black pepper
4 tablespoons paprika

1/2 tablespoon onion, minced
1/2 teaspoon cayenne pepper
1/2 teaspoon thyme
1/2 teaspoon oregano

Mix all ingredients and store in an airtight container.

Corn Pudding

1 #10 can creamed corn
1 cup sugar
12 eggs
1 teaspoon vanilla

1 quart half & half
1 cup flour
4 ounces margarine, melted

In a large mixing bowl, combine corn, sugar, eggs, vanilla, and half & half. Mix well. In a separate bowl, mix flour and margarine to form a paste. Add paste to pudding mixture. Pour mixture into baking pan and bake at 350 degrees for 20 minutes. Top should be golden brown. Serves 15.

Broiled Orange Roughy

10 ounces orange roughy filets
2 ounces Lemon Herb Butter*
1/2 teaspoon paprika

3 lemon slices
3 ounces rice pilaf
Parsley for garnish

Overlap filets on baking pan and broil for approximately 3 minutes. Remove from heat and pour herb butter over fish. Sprinkle with paprika, top with lemon slices, and return to broiler to finish cooking. Fish should be flaky. Drain butter into a side ramekin, place fish on a bed of rice pilaf, and garnish with parsley. Serves 1.

Lemon Herb Butter:
1/2 pound margarine
1/2 teaspoon black pepper
1 teaspoon thyme

1 teaspoon basil
1/2 teaspoon celery salt
1/4 cup lemon juice

Melt margarine in saucepan; add spices and lemon juice. Strain before using.

Hot Brown

2 slices white bread, toasted
2 ounces turkey, thinly sliced
2 ounces ham, thinly sliced
6 ounces white sauce
2 slices tomato

4 ounces cheddar cheese,
  shredded
2 strips bacon, cooked
1/2 ounce Parmesan cheese

Cut toast diagonally and arrange in skillet or heat-tempered platter. Heat turkey and ham; place on top of bread. Pour white sauce over top, covering bread and meat. Place tomato slices on top of gravy. Sprinkle cheddar cheese evenly on top. Melt cheese under broiler. Criss-cross bacon over cheddar cheese and sprinkle with Parmesan cheese. Place under broiler until Parmesan cheese browns lightly. Serves 1.

Entrée

Lamb Fries

12 to 14 ounces lamb fries
6 ounces white sauce

2 ounces cracker meal
Oil for deep-frying

Cut lamb fries lengthwise to the bottom of skin. Peel off skin. With flat side down on cutting board, begin slicing at short end. Cut slices 3/8-inch thick. Coat slices in cracker meal. Shake off excess meal and deep fry in 360-degree oil for approximately 4 minutes until crisp. Drain. Ladle white sauce onto large platter to cover entire bottom. Place fries on top of sauce. Serves 1.

Dessert

Black Forest Pie

1 pound unsalted butter
1 1/2 cups sugar
4 ounces unsweetened chocolate
1 tablespoon vanilla

4 eggs, room temperature
2 Oreo cookie pie crusts*
4 cups cherry pie filling
Whipped cream for topping

Melt butter in saucepan; remove from heat and blend in sugar. Melt chocolate in top of double boiler. Stir chocolate and vanilla into butter-sugar mixture. Allow to cool for 15 minutes. Using electric mixer, beat at high speed for 6 minutes. Mixture should be smooth and medium-brown in color.

In separate bowl, whip eggs until foamy. Fold eggs into batter. Evenly distribute batter into 2 pie crusts. Top each pie with cherry pie filling. Refrigerate for 3 hours before cutting. Top with whipped cream. Serves 12.

Oreo pie crust:
Oreo cookies, finely crushed
1/4 cup liquid margarine

Combine cookies and margarine. Pack bottoms, then sides of pie pans. Bake at 325 degrees for 2 minutes. Allow to cool 15 minutes before filling.

d.a. Clark's

There are so many things to love about d.a. Clark's. This new restaurant on the second floor of Chevy Chase Place has every perfect ingredient for a winning dining experience. You will know from your first visit that this will probably be your new "home away from home".

The extensive and varied menu is not to be believed! You could really eat there fifty times and not order the same delicious entrée twice. Diners who are fed up with skimpy, "nouveau" portions served at some restaurants, are delighted with the large servings at d.a. Clark's, and customers who want a light meal, find the à la carte menu a blessing. The prices are so reasonable, too, and you see budget-conscious college students side-by-side with professionals.

The decor at d.a. Clark's is definitely classy, with a comfortable, clubbish look and a warm, inviting feel. The owners explain that "the atmosphere, service and menu are meant to take you back to another time, one in which the portions were ample, the prices smaller and service relaxed and gracious." Diners are equally at home in evening wear or jeans, and your tastes could run from Grilled Lobster Tail to cheeseburgers. Large windows allow a lovely view of Chevy Chase, and there are wonderful patios where you may enjoy a drink or a full dinner.

There is culinary magic going on daily at d.a. Clark's. It's not magic that keeps you wanting to return-simply your good taste!

Owners: D. A. Clark
             P. F. Cotter
             Jamie Barr
             Tom Warren
Address: 836 Euclid (Chevy Chase Plaza)
             Lexington, Kentucky 40502
Telephone: (606) 266-1440 or 266-4707 (office)
Hours & Days: Monday-Saturday 11:30 am to 10:00 pm
                     Sunday 12:00 noon to 9:00 pm
                     Closed Thanksgiving and Christmas
Reservations recommended
Visa, MasterCard, American Express, Diner's Club
Directions: Second floor of Chevy Chase Plaza building.

d.a. Clark's

836 EUCLID, LEXINGTON   FEBRUARY 1990   Telephone 266-1440

SINCE 1989

APPETIZERS & COCKTAILS

French Onion	1.95
Soup Du Jour	2.50
Scallops Raymond	3.50
Stuffed Mushrooms	3.95
Imported Salami and Cheese	3.95
Beef & Shrimp Teriyaki Skewer	4.50
Sauteed Mushrooms	1.95
Calamari	3.25
Clams Casino (each) (min. 4)	.75
Baked Brie	5.95
Shrimp Cocktail	5.95
Oysters, halfshell (each) (min. 4)	.75
Oysters Remick (each (min. 4)	.95

FRESH PASTA & CASSOULET

Linguini with Clam	5.95
Linguini Aglio-Olio	5.95
Penne Bolognese	6.50
Penne Marinara	5.75
Shrimp Linguine Aglio-Olio	12.95
Mussels Marinara	8.95
Linguini Palermo	6.95
Scallop-Angel Hair	8.95
Pot Pie	4.95
Baked Penne	5.25
Pork Cassoulet	4.95
Frittata	3.25

STEAK, CHOPS & FOWL

New York (12 oz.)	7.95
Filet Mignon (6 oz.)	10.95
London Broil (8 oz.)	4.95
Lamb Chops (2 - 6 oz.)	12.95
Mixed Grill	14.95
Roast Duckling w/Orange Sauce	9.95
Roast Cornish Hen ½	3.25
Chicken Mediterranean	6.75
Chicken Breast Francaise	5.75
Roast NY w/Bearnais (Fri., Sat. Nights Only)	9.95

HOUSE SPECIALTIES

Veal Scallopine	10.95
Veal Saltimbocca	12.95
Mussels Dijonnaise	7.95
Chicken Wellington	9.95
Bouillabaisse	17.50
Pasta Fruite de Mer	15.95
Grilled Sweetbreads w/Madiera Sauce	12.95

SANDWICHES

Chicken Salad Sandwich	4.75
Grilled Chicken Sandwich	4.95
Marinated Pork Sandwich	4.25
Italian Sausage Sandwich	4.25
Veggie Sandwich	3.75
(w/cheese)	4.75
Steak Sandwich (8 oz. Strip)	4.95
Burger	3.95
(w/cheese)	4.25
Smoked Turkey	4.50
(w/cheese)	4.75

SIDES

Horseradish Sauce	.95
Forestierre Sauce	1.50
Burgandy Rosemary Sauce	1.25
Hollandaise	.95
Bearnaise	.95
Shallot and Caper Butter	.75
Garlic Butter	.75
Dill Butter	.75
Sour Cream	.50

VEGETABLES & POTATOES

Sauteed Mushrooms	1.95
Spaghetti Squash	.95
Glazed Carrots	1.25
Baked Acorn Squash	1.25
Eggplant Parmesian	1.95
Mixed Vegetables	1.25
Broccoli	1.25
Garlic Creamed Spinach	1.50
French Fries	.95
Oven Roasted Potatoes	1.50
Dilled New Potatoes	1.45
Au Gratin	2.25
Rice Pilaf	1.50

FRESH FISH & SEAFOOD

Grilled Tuna	9.95
Grilled Mahi Mahi	9.95
Grilled Salmon	11.95
Grilled Swordfish	12.95
Baked Scrod	7.95
Sole Grenoble	11.95
Seafood Mornay	9.95
Stuffed Calamari	4.95
Grilled Lobster Tail	17.95
Baked Scallops	10.95

SALADS

Garden Salad	1.95
Lettuce Wedge	1.00
Romaine with Anchovie Caper Vinaigrette	1.95
Chicken Tuscany	4.25
Sliced Beef and Romaine	4.50
Sliced Tomato, Cucumber and Onion	1.00
Mixed Winter Greens	1.95
Scallops, Mussels, Shrimp and Spinach w/Creamy Dill	4.95

DRESSINGS: Ranch, Raspberry Vinaigrette, Russian Olive Oil and Redwine Vinegar, Danish Bleu

DESSERTS

Flan	2.95
Strawberries Dolce	2.50
Key Lime Pie	2.95
French Vanilla Ice Cream	.95
(2 scoops)	1.75
Hot Fudge Sundae	2.95
Macadamia Nut Cheese Cake	3.95
Fruit Sundae	2.95
Chocolate Raspberry Terrine	4.25
Apple Pie	2.25
á la mode	2.95

SATURDAY & SUNDAY SPECIALS

Hangtown Fry (until 3 pm)	3.25
Frittata (always)	3.25
Eggs Benedict (until 3 pm)	5.95
Cheese Omelette (until 3 pm)	4.25
Steak, Egg & Hash Browns (until 3 pm)	6.50
Bacon, Egg & Hash Browns (until 3 pm)	4.50

WINE LIST

RED WINE

Geyser Peak	7.95
Thatcher Cabernet Sauvignon (FR)	9.95
North Coast Cellars Cabernet (US)	12.50
Cruse St. Emillion (FR)	17.50
Chateau Dillion 1985 (FR)	19.00
Vendange Cabernet Sauvignon 1985	8.95
St. Francis Merlot 1986	24.00
Rodney Strong Cabernet 1984	14.00
Cakebread Cabernet 1986	30.00
J.P. Mouiex St. Emillion 1985	18.50
Sutter Home Cabernet Sauvignon 1987	8.50
Clos du Bois Pinot Noir 1979	17.00
Chateau Coufran Bordeaux 1985 (FR)	18.00
Chateau Rausan Segla 1984	32.00
Corton Bressandes Burgundy 1981	38.00
Chianti (Wicker) 1987	12.95
Travaglini Gattinara (ITA)	23.00
Spring Mountain Cabernet Sauvignon 1983	12.75
Torres Cabernet	9.50
Chateau Beycheville 1985	65.00
Brouilly (Bouchard) 1987	16.50

WHITE WINE

Dore Sauvignon Blanc (US)	7.95
Thatcher Chardonnay (FR) (LTR)	9.95
Buena Vista Chardonnay (US)	14.50
Geyser Peak Chardonnay (US)	12.50
Geyser Peak Johannisberg Riesling (US)	9.75
Thorin Pouilly Fuisse (FR)	23.50
Torres Sauvignon Blanc	8.50
St. Francis Chardonnay 1987	16.00
Fontinelle Chardonnay 1987	17.00
Sartori Soave 1987	10.75
Louis Jadot Chassagne Montrachet 1985	48.00
Vendange Chardonnay 1987	8.95
Kenwood Dry Chenin Blanc 1987	11.95
Kenwood Johannisberg Riesling	12.75
Robert Young Chardonnay 1986	35.00
Belle Terre Chardonnay 1987	28.00
Sylvan Springs Sauvignon - Blanc 1986	7.95
San Angelo Pinot Grigio 1987	15.50
Santa Sofia Soave 1986	11.95
Monte Oilveto Vernaccia di San Gimignano (ITA)	13.50
Spring Mountain Chardonnay 1985	12.75
Oak Ridge Blanc de Blanc 1987	7.95
Puligny Montrachet (Bouchard) 1986	46.00
Simi Sauvignon Blanc	14.00

BLUSH

Kenwood White Zinfandel 1988	12.95
Vendange White Zinfandel 1988	8.95
Belvedere White Zinfandel (US)	7.95

ROSE

Chateau D'aqueria Tavel	18.00
Mateus	9.95

CHAMPAGNE & SPARKLING WINES

Weibel Brut (US)	9.95
Great Western Brut (US)	10.50
Barons Brut (US)	13.50
Piper Sonoma Brut	17.00
Chateau St. Jean 1985	18.50
Bricout Carte Noire (FR)	32.00
Perrier-Jouët Brut (FR)	45.00
Taittinger Blanc de Blanc 1983	110.00
Dom Perignon	115.00

MIXED DRINKS

Acapulco	3.50
Apple Rum Rickey	2.25
Bacardi Cocktail	2.25
Brandy Alexander	2.75
Bolero	3.50
Capri	2.75
Champagne Cocktail	2.75
Daiquiri	2.25
Martini	2.25
Manhattan	2.25
French 75	3.50
Imperial Fizz	2.25
Jack Rose	2.25
KIR	2.25
Long Island Ice Tea	3.50
Mai Tai	3.00
Movito	2.25
Old Fashioned	2.25
Ramos Fizz	2.75
Side Car	2.75
Tom Collins	2.25
Zombie	5.00
Typhoon	3.50
Screwdriver	2.25
Bloody Mary	2.25
Singapore Sling	3.50
Kentucky Cobbler	3.50
Hurricane	3.50
Margarita	2.75
All other drinks	1.95

BEERS

Watneys (UK)	3.50
Harp (IRE)	3.50
Simpatico (MEX)	3.00
Fishers LaBelle (FR)	3.50
Molson Canadian	3.00
Budweiser (US)	2.00
Becks (GER)	3.00
BudLight (US)	2.00
Coors (US)	2.00
Coors Light	2.00
Labatts (CAN)	3.00
Miller Lite (US)	2.00
Kirin Dry (Japan)	3.00
Swann (AUST)	3.00
Guiness (IRE)	3.00
Heineken (HOLL)	3.00
Amstel Light (HOLL)	3.00
Great Wall (China)	3.50

SOFT DRINKS

Coke, Sprite, Diet Coke, and Ginger Ale	.95
Ice Tea	.95
Milk	.95
Bottled Water	1.75
Root Beer	1.45
Coke (6 1/2 oz. Bottle)	1.10
Brewed Decaffeinated	.95
Expresso	1.00
Cappaccino	1.50
Orange, Tomato, Grapefruit	.95
Limeade	.95
Lemonade	.95

CORDIALS & AFTER DINNER

Irish Coffee	2.25
Spanish Coffee	2.75
Stinger	2.75
Gran Marnier	4.00
Black Russian	3.50
Tuaca	3.50
Chambord	3.50
Clocktower Port (Aust.)	2.00
Harveys Bristol Cream	3.25
Sandeman Royal Ambrosante Sherry	3.75
Warres Warrior Porto	3.25
Cockburn Sp. Reserve	3.25
Cockburn 20 yr. Tawny	4.50
Sandeman Dry Don Amontillado	3.25

Sandeman Maderia	3.25
Courvoisier VSOP	4.00
Armagnac De Montal VSOP	4.00
Asback "Uralt" (Germany)	3.50
Stock Grand Riserva 1984 (Ita.)	2.25
Hennessey VS	3.50
Sambuca	3.00
Tia Maria	3.00
Drambuie	3.50
Jagermeister	3.00
B & B	3.50
Benedictine	3.50
Delamain Cognac	4.00
Clark's Coffee	4.00

Pork Stuffed Mushrooms with Madeira Sauce

1/2 pound ground pork
4 tablespoons paprika
2 tablespoons thyme
3 tablespoons marjoram
Salt and pepper to taste
1 cup mushrooms, chopped
1/2 cup bread crumbs

2 eggs
1/4 cup Swiss cheese, grated
1/8 cup Parmesan cheese, grated
Chopped parsley
24 large mushroom caps
Madeira Sauce*

Sauté pork, add spices and cook until pork is done. Add chopped mushrooms and cook until tender. Remove from heat, add bread crumbs, eggs, cheeses, and parsley. Mix well. If mixture is not moist enough, add water to desired consistency. Fill mushroom caps and bake at 375 degrees for approximately 10 minutes. Serve with Madeira Sauce. Serves 4.

*Madeira Sauce:
1 cup Madeira
1/2 cup dry red wine
1 tablespoon shallots, chopped
1/2 garlic clove, chopped

2 cups veal or chicken stock
Parsley oil**
Salt and pepper to taste
2 1/2 tablespoons butter,
   room temperature

Boil Madeira, red wine, shallots and garlic in heavy saucepan until reduced to 1 1/2 tablespoons, approximately 15 minutes. Add stock and boil until reduced to 5 tablespoons, approximately 20 minutes; strain and set aside.

Add parsley oil and salt and pepper to sweetbreads, marinate 10 minutes. Cook until browned and slice diagonally. Reheat sauce, whisk in butter and spoon over sweetbreads.

**Parsley oil: Olive oil and chopped parsley

Chicken Tuscany

4 chicken breasts,
   boned and skinned
Oregano
Sage
Marjoram
Basil
Rosemary

Thyme
Mixed greens*
Italian Vinaigrette**
1/2 cup Parmesan cheese, grated
Roma tomatoes, sliced
Onions, julienned

Season chicken breasts with spices (1 pinch of each herb on each breast). Grill chicken breasts to desired doneness. Serve either hot or cool by slicing thinly and adding to mixed greens. Add Italian Vinaigrette slowly to mixed greens and chicken, tossing gently until coated. Sprinkle with Parmesan cheese. Place on tomato slices and onion. Serves 4.

* Endive, escarole, arugala, romaine or Boston lettuces
Use equal amounts of each, or substitute your favorite greens

**Italian Vinaigrette:*
1/2 cup red wine vinegar
1/2 cup olive oil
Fresh garlic, chopped
Fresh shallots, chopped
Worcestershire sauce
Tabasco sauce
2 tablespoons sugar
1 to 1 1/2 cups water
Salt and pepper to taste

Mix all ingredients together.

Baked Scallops

Entrée

2 pounds scallops
(preferably sea scallops)
1/2 pint heavy cream
1 tablespoon Worcestershire
sauce
Dash Tabasco sauce

2 tablespoons lemon juice
Bread crumbs
Parmesan cheese, grated
Paprika
Whole butter
Fresh parsley, chopped

Place scallops in baking dish; add cream, Worcestershire sauce, Tabasco, and lemon juice. Mix well. Add bread crumbs, a small amount at a time, mixing with a spoon. Mixture should be very moist but not soupy. Sprinkle remaining bread crumbs over the top. Add a sprinkling of Parmesan cheese; shake paprika over top for color and seasoning. Dot with butter and bake at 375 degrees until golden brown and bubbling. Garnish with chopped parsley. Serve 4.

Chicken Française

Entrée

4 1-ounce chicken breasts,
boned and skinned
Flour
4 to 5 tablespoons Parmesan
cheese, grated
3 eggs, beaten

Butter or oil for frying
1/2 cup fresh parsley, chopped
2 large lemons,
sectioned and chopped
1/4 pound whole butter, cubed
2 ounces dry white wine

Dredge chicken in flour. Combine Parmesan cheese with eggs; dip chicken into wash. Fry in hot skillet with butter or oil. When edges are browned, turn carefully. Remove from pan when fully cooked and discard cooking liquid. Add parsley, lemon, butter and white wine. Remove from heat and stir, making sure that butter does not separate. Pour sauce over chicken to serve. Serves 4.

Linguine with Clam Sauce

1/2 to 1 cup olive oil
2 tablespoons fresh garlic, chopped
6 ounces fresh (or frozen) clams, chopped
4 ounces fish or clam stock

4 pinches basil-oregano mix
3 ounces dry white wine
4 ounces fresh linguine
Parmesan cheese, grated
Chopped parsley, small handful

In hot skillet, add olive oil and garlic. Before garlic starts to brown, add clams and clam juice. Season with spices; pour in white wine and reduce by 1/3. Place fresh linguine into pot of boiling, salted water; cook until al denté, approximately 2 to 3 minutes. Drain and add to clam sauce. Remove from heat, add Parmesan cheese and parsley. Toss and serve with tongs. Serve remaining clams and sauce over linguine. Serves 1.

Sole Grenoble

8 sole filets, 2 to 4 ounces each
Flour
4 eggs, beaten
1 bunch parsley, chopped

4 tablespoons capers
2 lemons, sectioned
8 ounces whole butter, cubed

Dredge sole in flour, dip in egg, and place in hot skillet with butter or oil. Turn when sole starts to brown around the edges. Remove from pan when fully cooked and discard cooking liquid. Add parsley, capers, lemon sections and butter. Ingredients must be added in order listed, making sure not to burn or break butter sauce. Serves 4.

Veal Saltimboca

Veal
1 pound prosciutto, thinly sliced
Leaf sage
Flour

1/2 teaspoon shallots, chopped
40 mushrooms, quartered
16 ounces marsala wine
Chopped Parsley

Slice veal and pound evenly with mallet until almost translucent when held to light. Weight should be 1 ounce per slice. Place a thin slice of prosciutto and leaf sage on veal; fold veal scallopini and repound with mallet. Dredge in flour and sauté. Remove from pan, discarding oil. Add shallots and mushrooms; deglaze with marsala. Finish with parsley. Serves 4.

deSha's

Desha's restaurant and Bar opened in 1985 on the corner of Main and Broadway. Way back in the 1870's, during a period of booming prosperity for Lexington, the present structure that houses deSha's was built for commercial use. Through the years it served as a grocery, general store, basket factory, and furniture mart. DeSha's, and in fact the whole city block in this historic section of Lexington, has been beautifully restored to its former glory. Named Victorian Square, it is today a shopping mall that is listed with the National Registry.

DeSha's is spread out over two stories, and offers a view of downtown and Triangle Park. Decorated in warm tones of burgundy, blue, and green, deSha's captures the feel of an elegant, but comfortable, home. Photos of Lexington and its citizens during the nineteenth century adorn the walls as another reminder of its interesting past.

This friendly, Victorian rendezvous features some of the best food around and at reasonable prices. In addition to fresh, crunchy salads, sandwiches, soups and vegetables, there is a long list of entrées such as Steak deSha, Seafood Fettuccine, and Chicken Monterey. DeSha's serves a delicious hot loaf of southern-style cornbread with their entrées. Made with sour cream and cream-style corn, it is moist and wonderful drizzled with honey butter.

After dinner, wander over to deSha's Main Cross Tavern, named for the streets Main and Main Cross before they became Main and Broadway. Exposed brick walls, high ceilings, and overhead street lamps create a perfect atmosphere for friendly conversation. An old Wurlitzer jukebox, converted to play compact discs, along with live entertainment from soft rock to jazz are part of Main Cross Tavern's appeal.

Dinner at deSha's invites lingering long into the night for some, and just dropping by for others, but simply everyone enjoys their stay.

Owner: Nick Sanders
     WNS, Inc.
Address: 101 North Broadway
     Lexington, Kentucky 40507
Telephone: (606) 259-3771
Hours & Days: Dining: Monday-Thursday 11:00 am to 11:00 pm
     Friday-Saturday 11:00 am to midnight
     Sunday 11:00 am to 10:00 pm
     Sunday Brunch 11:00 am to 2:00 pm
     Bar: Monday-Saturday 11:00 am to 1:00 am
     Sunday 11:00 am to 11:00 pm
Reservations not required
Visa, MasterCard, American Express, Diner's Club, Carte Blanche
Directions: Downtown Lexington, corner of Main Street and Broadway.

Appetizers

Buffalo Chicken Wings
Seasoned hot, medium, or mild
12 for 3.75   25 for 6.95

Coconut Chicken
with honey mustard sauce
5.75

Wings and Rings
5.95

Stuffed Mushrooms
Filled with crabmeat and cream cheese
6.75

Calamari Sauté
Tender squid steak sautéed in herb butter
5.95

French Onion Soup
3.50

Stuffed Banana Peppers
Stuffed with mozzarella cheese. Served
with marinara sauce.
5.95

Chilled Shrimp
6 for 5.75   13 for 10.95

Potato Skins   **Onion Rings**
5.25   4.95

Sandwiches & Salads

Hot Brown
Sliced Turkey covered with cream sauce,
topped with cheddar cheese, bacon and
tomato. Served with dinner salad.
8.95

Half Pound Burger
with natural fries and cole slaw
5.25   cheese add .50

Steak Sandwich
Petite filet, with natural fries
and cole slaw
8.25

Fried Chicken
with natural fries and cole slaw
9.95

All our dressings are made fresh in-house and include:
French, Italian, Creamy Herb, Bleu Cheese, and 1000 Island.

House Salad
A mixture of iceberg, bibb, and romaine
lettuce topped with mushrooms, carrots,
tomatoes, cucumbers, chopped egg,
and red onion. Served with cornbread
and honey butter.
5.95   cheddar cheese add .50

Spinach Salad
Served with cornbread and honey butter
6.25

From The Grill

Served with a warm loaf of deShá's own special cornbread and honey butter, dinner salad and a choice of
baked potato, sweet potato, natural fries or wild rice.

Roasted Prime Rib Au Jus
12 oz. 14.50   16 oz. 16.50

Steak deShá
Tenderloin chunks seasoned
in a special marinade
13.95

New York Strip
Peppercorn sauce
15.95

Filet Mignon
Garlic butter
14.95

Filet & Shrimp
Petite filet and lightly breaded shrimp
13.95

Chicken Monterey
Grilled chicken and sun dried tomatoes
in a white wine sauce
13.95

Twin Lamb Chops
Bernaise, mint jelly
14.95

Pork Loin Filet
Barbecue sauce
12.50

Grilled Lemon Pepper Chicken
12.95

Breasts of Barbecue Chicken
11.95

Seafood

Served with cornbread and honey butter and dinner salad

Fresh Catch of the Day
We order limited quantities of fish and
seafood to guarantee freshness and
high quality in every dish we prepare.
Check with your server for today's
catch and market price.

Seafood Fettucine
Bay shrimp and scallops, crabmeat,
and fettucine in a sherry lobster sauce
14.50

Jumbo Charbroiled Shrimp
In garlic butter with wild rice, parmesan tomato
14.50

Deep Fried Gulf Shrimp
With choice of baked potato, sweet potato,
natural fries or wild rice
12.95

Sweet Potato Muffins

4 eggs
2 cups self-rising flour
1/2 tablespoon baking soda
1/2 tablespoon baking powder
2 teaspoons cinnamon
1 1/2 cups vegetable oil

2 cups sugar
2 cups sweet potatoes,
 cooked and mashed
1 cup crushed pineapple
3/4 cup pecans, chopped

Beat eggs separately. Mix flour, baking soda, baking powder, and cinnamon together. In a separate bowl, cream oil and sugar. Add eggs and sweet potatoes; mix well. Stir in dry ingredients, pineapple, and pecans. Mix well and pour into greased muffin pans, filling to the rim. Bake at 350 degrees for approximately 20 minutes. Makes 24 muffins.

Hawaiian Chicken Salad

3 cups cooked chicken,
 white meat
1 1/2 cups pineapple tidbits

1 1/4 cups mayonnaise
2 green onions, diced
3/4 cup pecans, chopped

Dice chicken into large chunks. Add remaining ingredients and mix well. Serves 6.

Squash Casserole

3 large summer squash
3 large zucchini
2 large onions
1/2 tablespoon salt
2 2/3 cups water
1 1/2 cups butter, melted
3/4 teaspoon pepper

1/2 cup + 2 tablespoons sugar
12 eggs
1/2 tablespoon soy sauce
5 cups cheddar cheese, grated
3 cups Ritz cracker crumbs
3/4 teaspoon paprika

Slice squash and zucchini; cook with onions and salt in water until tender enough to mash. Mash and add melted butter, pepper, sugar, eggs, soy sauce, 3 cups cheese, and 2 cups cracker crumbs. Mix well. Pour into greased 9 x 13 inch pan. Top with remaining cheese and cracker crumbs. Sprinkle with paprika and bake at 350 degrees for approximately 25 minutes. Serves 12.

Note: You may use 6 large zucchini or 6 large yellow squash instead of a combination of the two.

Sweet Potato Casserole

3/4 cup butter, melted
1 cup sugar
4 eggs
2 1/4 teaspoons vanilla
Dash cinnamon
Dash allspice

2/3 cup whipping cream
1/2 teaspoon salt
6 cups sweet potatoes, cooked,
  peeled and mashed
  (5 large sweet potatoes)
Topping*

Cream butter and sugar. Add eggs, vanilla, spices, cream and salt. Fold sweet potatoes into mixture; blend well. Pour into greased 9 x 13 inch pan and cover with topping. Bake at 350 degrees for approximately 20 minutes. Serves 12.

*Topping:
1/2 cup + 2 tablespoons butter
1 cup brown sugar
1/2 cup + 2 tablespoons flour
1 cup pecans, chopped

Melt butter; add sugar, flour and pecans. Mix well.

Lemon Ice Box Pie

3 eggs
1/3 teaspoon salt
1 1/3 cans sweetened
  condensed milk

3/4 cup lemon juice
1 9-inch graham cracker crust

Beat eggs; add salt, milk, and lemon juice. Mix well, pour into pie crust and bake at 350 degrees for approximately 15 minutes. Chill several hours before serving. Serves 6 to 8.

Dudley's Restaurant

Ask anyone in Lexington for a list of their favorite restaurants, and Dudley's is sure to be mentioned every time. This extremely popular restaurant is a hit with everybody. Chic, but friendly and unpretentious, Dudley's has an outstanding menu and wonderfully prepared food. No wonder it's so well liked!

Dudley's Restaurant is located in a one hundred year old school house. In 1979, the school was renovated to house shops and in 1981, Dudley's Restaurant was added by converting two of the original classrooms into a bar and dining room. In 1983, an outdoor courtyard was added, where lunch and dinner are served under tulip poplar trees as old and beautiful as the building itself.

Owners Debbie Long and John Shea have created a restaurant which perfectly reflects the building, as well as the historic South Hill section in which they are located. Decorated with soft mauves and greens, the walls are filled with local artists' works. A century old bar from Paris, Kentucky's Smokehouse Pool Room finds a perfect home at Dudley's.

The Continental menu at Dudley's features the freshest beef, veal, seafood, pasta, and vegetables. Pasta Dudley-Style (a popular entrée with regulars) is a mélange of chicken, sun-dried tomatoes, and vegetables, tossed in angel hair pasta, white wine and Parmesan cheese.

Locals and visitors to Lexington always return to Dudley's. This will probably become one of your favorites, too! See you there!

Owners: Debbie Long and John Shea
Address: 380 South Mill Street
Lexington, Kentucky 40508
Telephone: (606) 252-1010
Hours & Days: Lunch: 11:30 am to 2:30 pm daily
Dinner: Sunday-Thursday 5:30 pm to 10:00 pm
Friday-Saturday 5:30 pm to 11:00 pm
Reservations recommended for dinner only
Visa, MasterCard, American Express
Directions: Corner of Maxwell and South Mill Streets,
1 1/2 blocks from downtown Hyatt Regency and
Radisson Hotels.

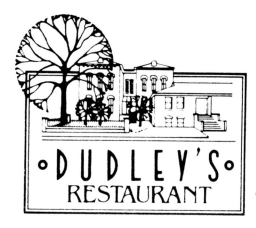

Appetizers

Oysters on the half shell   4.95

Oysters baked with Brie and bacon   5.50

Crab Cakes with chile mayonnaise   6.25

Green Chile Wontons with salsa   4.50

Quesadillas with pico de gallo   4.50

Crab Puff - *puff pastry filled with crabmeat and gruyere cheese, baked and topped with hollandaise*   4.25

* Artichoke - *steamed and served whole*   4.50

Baked Brie - *in a puff pastry, served with fresh fruit*   3.95

Fettucine Alfredo   3.95

Lobster Fettucine   6.75

Cajun Grilled Shrimp   6.25

Spicy Chicken Fingers *with a confetti sauce*   5.50

Soups & Salads

Soups of the Day - *Cup* 1.50
Bowl 2.25

Spinach and Shrimp Salad - *served with a sweet and sour poppyseed dressing*   5.25
1/2 order   3.50

Avocado, Grapefruit, and Lump Crab Salad - *served with a sweet and sour popyseed dressing*   6.50

*Greek Style Salad - *feta cheese, zucchini; artichoke hearts, tomatoes, and black olives*   5.50   *1/2 order* 3.75

Pasta

Pasta Primavera - *a concoction of seafood, vegetables, and cheese*   10.50

* Pasta Dudley's Style - *chicken, sundried tomatoes, and vegetables tossed with an angel hair pasta and a hint of fennel*   11.95

Angel Hair Pasta with Shrimp & Scallops - *fresh spinach, sundried tomatoes, pinenuts, and lemon pepper*   13.95

Pasta - *created nightly MKT.*

* These items can be prepared lower in salt, cholesterol and fat, as recommended by the American Heart Association.

Chicken & Seafood

*Grilled Marinated Chicken Breast - *served with grilled vegetables*   *9.95*

Chicken Milano - *stuffed with proscuitto ham and herbed cream cheese served with a port wine sauce*   *12.95*

Chicken Galadriel - *sauteed chicken breast served on angel hair pasta with broccoli and parmesan cheese*   *13.95*

Chicken Livers Normandy - *sauteed with apples, bacon, and brandy*   *8.95*

Large Sea Scallops - *in garlic butter*   *10.95*

Grilled Swordfish - *served with your choice of herb butter or chef's special sauce*   *MKT*

Fresh Fish or Seafood - *when superior selection available, grilled, blackened, or broiled*   *MKT*

Beef & Veal

Tournedos Maxwell - *small filets crowned with crabmeat and bearnnaise sauce*   *15.95*

Filet of Beef - *grilled plain or served with a mushroom bordelaise*   *15.95*

N.Y. Strip - *served with broccoli and baked potato*   *13.95*

Tenderloin and Shrimp - *tenderloin tips sauteed in lemon pepper cream sauce and served with two fresh shrimp*   *14.95*

Veal Francaise - *Scallopini of veal sauteed in a white wine cream sauce*   *13.50*

Veal Cornett - *Provimi veal sauteed in a dijon cream sauce*   *13.95*

*Dudley's is proud to offer a selection of specials daily,
along with fresh baked muffins and breads*

Spicy Chicken Fingers
With Confetti Sauce

8 chicken breasts
2 cups bread crumbs
1 tablespoon chili powder
1 teaspoon cumin
1 teaspoon cayenne pepper
1 teaspoon black pepper

1 tablespoon crushed red pepper
1 teaspoon garlic
2 eggs
2 tablespoons milk
Vegetable oil

Confetti Sauce:
13 ounces honey
1 tablespoon crushed red pepper

1 teaspoon garlic
1/2 ounce Tabasco sauce

Cut chicken breasts into strips and set aside. Combine bread crumbs with spices and set aside. Beat eggs with milk. Dip chicken in egg mixture, then in spiced crumb mixture. Fry pieces in hot oil and drain on paper towels. Mix all ingredients for sauce together in a bowl. Serve fingers hot with sauce on the side. Serves 6 to 8.

Tomato-Dill Soup
With Sour Cream

6 cups diced onions
2 sticks butter
1 tablespoon garlic, chopped
1/4 cup + 1 teaspoon flour
2 24-ounce cans whole
  plum tomatoes

2 to 4 cups chicken stock
  or water
3 bay leaves
1 teaspoon thyme
1 tablespoon sugar
2 cups sour cream

Sweat onions in butter, cooking until soft but not brown. Add garlic halfway through cooking of onions. Stir in enough flour to make a thick paste. Cook for 10 minutes over low heat, stirring constantly to prevent browning. Set aside for 10 minutes.

Crush tomatoes by hand. Add tomatoes, stock, bay leaves, thyme and sugar to thickened sauce. Stir well. Simmer slowly for 40 minutes, stirring occasionally to prevent sticking. Add more stock if necessary. Allow soup to cool 15 minutes. In a food processor, add a small amount of soup with sour cream and blend. Quickly whisk sour cream and soup mixture into the remaining soup. Add fresh dill. Serves 8 to 10.

Dudley's Muffins

2 cups flour
1/4 cup sugar
Pinch of salt
3 teaspoons baking powder
1 1/4 cups milk

1/4 cup dark corn syrup
1/4 cup butter, melted
1/4 cup fresh berries, raisins,
 or nuts
Cinnamon or nutmeg to taste

Preheat oven to 350 degrees. Mix all ingredients by hand in order listed, being extremely careful not to overmix. Bake in muffin pans for 12 minutes or until done. Makes 12 muffins.

Pasta Dudley's Style

2 1/2 pounds capellini
Olive oil
3 pounds chicken breasts,
 skinned and boned
Salt and pepper to taste
12 ounces clarified butter*
6 ounces carrots, thinly sliced

1 1/2 medium red onions,
 thinly sliced
4 ounces sun-dried tomatoes**
Juice of 2 lemons
1 to 1 1/2 cups white wine
6 ounces frozen peas
6 ounces Parmesan cheese,
 grated

Cook pasta in boiling salted water. Drain and cool. Toss with small amount of olive oil; set aside.

Cut chicken breasts into strips; salt and pepper lightly. Using clarified butter*, sauté in hot skillet on both sides. Add carrots, red onions, and sun-dried tomatoes**. Quickly sauté in pan with chicken. Deglaze pan with lemon juice and white wine. Add peas; toss in pasta to warm. Serve with grated Parmesan cheese. Serves 6.

*To clarify butter: Simmer butter and skim off the foamy white matter that comes to surface. Carefully separate the clarified butter from the milk solids that settle to the bottom.

**Sun-dried tomatoes may be purchased packed in oil, in which case you separate the oil from the tomatoes. If purchased dried, plump overnight in a solution of 5% vinegar to water; slice into thin strips.

Entrée

Veal Cornett

1 1/2 to 2 pounds veal cutlets
Salt and pepper to taste
Flour
12 ounces clarified butter
3 cups heavy cream
3 ounces dry white wine
2 tablespoons Dijon mustard

1 tablespoon dried tarragon
  (or 2 tablespoons
  fresh tarragon)
1 tablespoon dried basil
  (or 2 tablespoons
  fresh basil)
Fresh butter, cold

Pound veal between two pieces of wax paper. Lightly salt and pepper. Dredge with flour and shake off excess. Sauté cutlets in hot pan using clarified butter. Remove veal onto plate, drain excess fat; deglaze pan with white wine. Reduce, add cream; reduce again and add mustard, tarragon, and basil. Adjust salt and pepper, if necessary. Finish with fresh butter, if desired. Serve with fresh pasta and vegetables of your choice. Serves 6.

Dessert

French Chocolate Cake

3 ounces semi-sweet chocolate
3 ounces unsweetened chocolate
1 1/2 sticks butter
1 1/2 cups sugar
6 eggs

2 ounces Grand Marnier
1 1/2 cups ground almonds
1/3 cup bread crumbs
1 teaspoon baking soda

Glaze:
3 ounces unsweetened chocolate

4 tablespoons butter
2 tablespoons honey

Preheat oven to 350 degrees. Melt chocolate in double boiler, then cool. Cream butter with sugar. Add eggs, one at a time, beating well after each addition. Add Grand Marnier, almonds, bread crumbs and baking soda. Whisk by hand until just mixed. Pour into a lightly buttered and floured springform pan. Bake 40 to 50 minutes or until toothpick inserted in center comes out dry.

For glaze: Melt chocolate, butter and honey in double boiler. Cool until thick. Spread thin layer over cooled cake. Serves 8.

fleur-de-lys

On a side street in downtown Lexington is a tiny French restaurant causing a big commotion. Fleur-de-lys has all the ambiance and charm of a New York City bistro, and the warmth and welcome of a small town café.

Fleur-de-lys' owner, John Ferguson, brings a decade of experience in the restaurant business to this venture, as well as an innate love of food and a keen sense of the pleasures of the table. The menu, written in both French and English, is made up of regional French specialties, which John Ferguson describes as more "country French than haute cuisine". His own special touch makes the tried and true French dishes even more delicious.

The cozy dining room is opened up by mirrored walls and windows that face busy downtown pedestrians. A small bar overlooks one of those large shiny brass capuccino machines, and a cup of Espresso or Capuccino tastes so nice after a dinner of Suprême de Caneton aux Cerises Sèches or Coquilles St. Jacques Persillade.

On Monday nights, fleur-de-lys is closed to the public, but available for private parties. Because of its size, this is an ideal spot for a dinner party, a birthday celebration, or just a gathering of friends who enjoy fine dining.

Fleur-de-lys has the wonderful combination of great food, conscientious service, and attention to detail that makes for a delightful restaurant.

Owner: John Ferguson
Address: 120 South Upper
Lexington, Kentucky 40507
Telephone: (606) 252-7946
Hours & Days: Dinner: Tuesday-Thursday 6:00 pm to 10:00 pm
Friday-Saturday 6:00 pm to 10:30 pm
Reservations recommended
Visa, MasterCard, American Express
Directions: Downtown Lexington, 1 block off Main Street on South Upper.

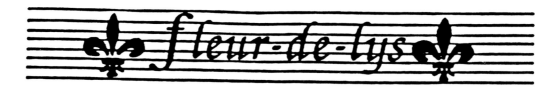

french regional specialties

Appetizers

Terrine Maison 5⁵⁰
Baked Páte of Pork, Veal, Liver & Walnuts, flavored with Cognac.
Saumon Fumé 7⁰⁰
Thinly sliced Nova Scotia Salmon with Cream Cheese and Caviar.
Escargots au Porto 6⁰⁰
Sauteed with Garlic and Mushrooms, Deglazed with Port Wine and Served
Over Angel Hair Pasta.
Brochette de Crevettes et Pétoncles 7⁰⁰
Skewered Shrimp and Scallops with Ginger Aioli.
Croûte `d' Huitres Rémoulade 6⁰⁰
Pan Fried Oysters in Spicy Caper Mayonnaise.
Tempeh a l'orientale 6⁰⁰
Toasted Soybean Cake with Stir-fried Vegetables.

Soupe de Saison 3⁵⁰   *Oyster Bisque* 4²⁵

Entrees

Poissons frais du Jour .... *Market*
Fresh Fish of the Day

Coquilles St. Jacques Persillade *14⁰⁰*
Sauteed Sea Scallops in Parsley & Garlic

Pate aux Fruits de Mer *15⁰⁰*
An Array of Fresh Seafood in a Sun Dried Tomato Cream Over Fresh Ribbon Pasta.

Suprême de Caneton aux Cerises Seches *16⁰⁰*
Roast Breast ofDuckling with Sauce of Sun-Dried Cherries, Kirsch.

Suprême de Volaille "UFO" *12⁵⁰*
Sauteed Breast of Chicken Garnished with Mushrooms, Roast Garlic and Gruyére.

Rôti de Filet de Porc Moûtarde *15⁰⁰*
Oven-Roasted Pork Tenderloin with a Dijon Mustard Crust

Cotes d' Agneau `a l' Ail Roti *18⁵⁰*
Grilled Lamb Chops with Whole Roasted Garlic

Filet de Boeuf Valois *17⁵⁰*
Grilled Beef Tenderloin with Demi-glace-enhanced Bearnaise

Desserts ask your server for today's selections

°15% gratuity added to parties of 7 or more   *NO CIGARS, PLEASE!

°Restaurant is available Monday nights for Private Parties.

Gridded Goat Cheese

2 cups red cabbage,
  finely shredded
Butter to sauté
2 ounces heavy cream
Salt and pepper to taste

3 tablespoons clarified butter
8 ounces goat cheese*
2 eggs, beaten
1/2 cup flour
Chopped parsley for garnish

Sauté red cabbage in butter and moisten with cream. Season with salt and pepper.

Heat butter in sauté pan. Slice goat cheese into 4 slices. Dip in egg wash, then dredge in flour. Sauté until golden brown on both sides. Place on bed of warmed red cabbage and garnish with chopped parsley. Serves 4.

*log shaped, Chevron is preferred

Oyster Stew

3 tablespoons green end of
  scallion, thinly sliced
2 tablespoons butter
16 to 20 oysters with liquid
1/4 teaspoon lobster butter*
2 teaspoons Worcestershire sauce

2 dashes Tabasco sauce
2 cups half and half
1/4 cup heavy cream
Salt and black pepper to taste
Parsley to garnish

Sauté scallions in butter over medium heat for 30 seconds. Add oysters and cook 1 minute or until edges start to curl. Add lobster butter, Worcestershire sauce, Tabasco sauce, half and half, and cream. Season to taste. Heat until bubbly. Garnish with chopped parsley and serve. Serves 4.

*Sauté lobster or shrimp shells and onion in 1 stick butter. Pour brandy over, reduce, and strain.

Winter Root Soup

White part of 1 leek, julienned
2 tablespoons butter
2 1/2 cups chicken broth
1 large beet, julienned
2 carrots, peeled and julienned
1 large parsnip or turnip,
  peeled and julienned

1 large potato,
  peeled and julienned
1/2 cup sour cream
Chopped parsley for garnish

Sauté leek in butter. Add broth and bring to a boil. Stir in vegetables and simmer 30 minutes. Mix 3 tablespoons of soup broth with sour cream. Garnish soup with a spoonful of sour cream and chopped parsley. Serves 4.

Caesar Salad Bonne Femme
(Steak Salad)

1 head Romaine lettuce,
   washed, dried, and chilled
Caesar Dressing*
1 cup croutons

1/4 cup grated Parmesan cheese
8-ounce grilled sirloin or
   tenderloin, chilled
Pepper, freshly ground

Toss Romaine with dressing, croutons, and most of the cheese, saving some for garnish. Cut sirloin into thin slices and top with remaining Parmesan. Finish with more freshly ground pepper. Serves 4.

*Caesar Dressing
2 cloves garlic, finely minced
2 anchovies,
   mashed with above garlic
Juice of 1 lemon
Dash Worcestershire sauce

Dash Tabasco sauce
2 egg yolks
1 cup olive oil
Pepper, freshly ground

Whisk ingredients together.

Potato Gratin Savoyarde

6 Idaho potatoes,
   peeled and thinly sliced
1 cup chicken broth

1 cup heavy cream
Salt and black pepper to taste
1 cup Gruyère cheese, grated

Layer potato slices in baking dish, allowing a large surface area. Layer should be no more than 1 1/2 inches thick. Add broth, heavy cream, and season. Top with cheese. Bake at 375 degrees for 1 hour. Serves 4.

Roast Duck Breast
With Sun-Dried Cherries and Kirsch

4 duck breasts, boneless,
   skins intact, 8 to 10 ounces each
1 small leek, julienned

3 tablespoons sun-dried cherries
1/2 cup demi-glaze
1/4 cup kirsch

Preheat oven to 400 degrees. Place duck breasts on rack and roast for 20 minutes. In pie pan, make a bed of leeks and cherries and place duck on bed. Pour demi-glaze and kirsch over the top. Broil 6 to 8 minutes, or until duck is medium rare. Slice duck and cover with sauce. Serves 4.

Seafood Pasta

White of 1 leek, julienned
1 carrot, julienned
3 tablespoons clarified butter
12 jumbo shrimp
16 sea scallops
4 2-ounce salmon filet pieces
4 lobster pieces, tails or claws

1/2 cup white wine
1 cup heavy cream
2 ounces sun-dried tomatoes,
    julienned
Salt and white pepper to taste
1/2 to 1 pound fresh pasta
    (fettuccine)

Sauté leek and carrot in butter. Add seafood and under cook. Add white wine and cream. Remove seafood and keep warm. Add sun-dried tomatoes, season and reduce over high heat for 3 to 4 minutes. Add seafood and cook only until heated. Serve over pasta. Serves 4.

Beignets
(French Doughnuts)

1 cup water
1/2 cup butter
1 cup flour
Pinch salt

Pinch nutmeg
1/2 teaspoon baking powder
4 eggs
Powdered sugar

In sauce pan, bring water and butter to a boil. Add flour all at once, stirring with a wooden spoon until all lumps are incorporated. Add salt, nutmeg, and baking powder. With a mixer, beat in eggs, one at a time. Fry in 350-degree oil until doubled in bulk. Increase heat to 375 degrees and fry until golden brown. Dust with powdered sugar.

Gratz Park Inn

Gratz Park Inn, a small hotel in the heart of downtown Lexington, offers the elegance, comfort and warmth of a fine old manor home. A renovation of a 1917 historic landmark, "The Lexington Clinic", the hotel opened in the late summer of 1987 and filled a need in Lexington for luxury downtown accommodations.

From the first week of operation, the elegant dining room at Gratz Park Inn has achieved recognition as one of Lexington's finest. The restaurant has become a favorite spot for breakfast, lunch, dinner or late night supper. The culinary genius of Chef Patrick Taylor is supported by an impeccable service staff. Sunday brunch is extremely popular, too, and one visit tells you why. Basted Eggs El Paso or Grilled Tomato and Smoked Gouda Omelet share the menu with Grilled New York Strip and Eggs Benedict, to name but a few tempting brunch items.

The excellent cuisine at Gratz Park Inn can also be part of business meetings or private parties, either in one of their lovely banquet rooms, or off the premises entirely.

Gratz Park Inn is such a pleasure for its intimate, relaxed setting and emphasis on warmth and graciousness. They have also become a first-rate dining establishment. The motto at the Inn is "Quite simply, first class everything."

Address: 120 West Second Street
Lexington, Kentucky 40507
Telephone: (606) 231-6666 or 1-800-227-4362
Hours & Days: Breakfast: Sunday-Saturday 6:30 am to 11:00 am
Lunch & Sunday Brunch: 11:00 am to 2:30 pm
Dining Room: Sunday-Thursday 5:30 pm to 10:00 pm
Friday-Saturday 5:30 pm to 10:30 pm
Reservations recommended
Visa, MasterCard American Express, Diners Club, Carte Blanche
Directions: Down North Limestone, turn left onto West 2nd Street;
downtown Lexington.

DINNER

Soup of the Day   2.50
Chicken Gumbo   3.00

* * *

Caesar Salad with Fresh Parmesan Cheese   3.00
Mixed Green Salad with Pine Nuts and Roast Shallot Dressing   3.00
Cucumber, Tomato and Bibb Lettuce with Basil Vinaigrette   3.00

* * *

Shrimp and Crabmeat Cocktail   6.50
Steamed Mussels with Basil Beurre Blanc   6.00
Louisiana Lump Crab Cakes with Red Pepper Mayonnaise   6.25
Smoked Salmon and Potato Pancake   8.25

* * *

Grilled New York Strip with Bourbon Sauce   18.50
Roast Duckling with Apple Butter - Brandy Sauce   16.00
Grilled Mahi-Mahi with Shrimp and Mushrooms   16.45
Sauteed Twin Fillets with Wild Mushrooms and Madiera   19.50
Grilled Breast of Chicken with Red Pepper Mayonaise and Scallions   13.00
Grilled Veal Chop with Orange Cream   20.50
Marinated Tuna Steak with Onions, Peppers and Avocados   16.00
Lamb Loin with Rosemary Mint Glace   18.50
Sauteed Shrimp with Black and White Pasta   18.50
Mixed Grill: Chef's Selections   20.00

Baked Idaho Potato Available
The Above Items May Be Prepared To Your Personal Taste Upon Request

Desserts

Fresh Strawberries in Grand Marnier Creme a' l' Anglaise 3.75

*Freshly picked berries smothered in a cream sauce
flavored with vanilla and Grand Marnier*

Creme Caramel 3.25

A light vanilla custard with Caramel Sauce

White Chocolate Mousse Puff 4.00

*A light cream puff filled with White Chocolate Mousse
on Raspberry Sauce*

Chocolate Raspberry Cheesecake 4.25

Dense and decadent

Bourbon Pecan Pie 3.75

Our version of a traditional favorite

Chocolate Truffle Loaf 3.75

A chocolate lovers delight accented in a raspberry sauce.

Ice Creams

French Vanilla 3.25
Milk Chocolate and Banana 3.25
Butterfinger and Vanilla 3.25
Coffee Amaretto 3.25

Smoked Salmon and Potato Pancake

2 large baking potatoes, cooked,
  peeled and grated
2 tablespoons caraway seed
3 green onions, chopped
2 teaspoon salt

1/2 teaspoon black pepper
1/4 cup oil
8 ounces sour cream
8 ounces smoked salmon,
  thinly sliced

Combine first 5 ingredients and divide into 4 portions. Lightly coat omelet pan with oil and heat over medium-high flame. Sauté potatoes until brown on both sides. Coat with sour cream and cover with salmon. Warm lightly under broiler and serve. Serves 4.

Cream of Broccoli with Smoked Gouda

4 ounces butter
1 small onion, chopped
1 bunch broccoli stems,
  chopped, florets reserved
4 ounces flour

32 ounces chicken stock
8 ounces smoked gouda, grated
8 ounces cream
Salt to taste
White pepper to taste

Melt butter in heavy-bottomed saucepan. Add onion and broccoli stems; sauté until onion is translucent. Add flour and stir until a light paste forms. Cook over low heat approximately 2 minutes. Stir in chicken stock; simmer over medium heat 15 minutes. Blend in cheese, stirring until melted. Strain, reserving broth and discarding vegetables. Soup should be kept hot. Add cream and broccoli florets 15 minutes before serving, correcting seasonings if needed. Serves 8.

Chicken Salad with Walnuts and Dill

24 ounces chicken meat,
cleaned and cooked
4 stalks celery, minced
6 green onions, minced
18 small broccoli florets,
blanched

2 ounces walnuts, chopped
1 ounce lemon juice
1 teaspoon fresh dill, chopped
2 cups mayonnaise
Salt and white pepper to taste

Combine all ingredients except mayonnaise, salt and pepper. Mix thoroughly, being careful to leave chicken in bite-size pieces. Fold in mayonnaise and correct seasonings. Serves 8.

Sautéed Sole with Tomato Caper Butter

1 stick butter, softened
1/2 tomato, peeled,
seeded and chopped
1 tablespoon capers
1 teaspoon garlic, chopped
Juice of 1 lemon
1/2 teaspoon salt

1/4 teaspoon black pepper
1 tablespoon parsley, chopped
4 6-ounce sole filets,
seasoned with salt and pepper
4 ounces vegetable oil
8 ounces flour
6 eggs, lightly beaten

Combine butter, tomato, capers, garlic, lemon juice, salt, pepper and parsley; blend well. Heat oil in heavy-bottomed sauté pan until very hot. Dredge sole filets in flour and dip in egg wash. Take filets directly from egg wash and place skin side up in sauté pan; cook 1 minute or until lightly browned. Turn, reduce heat, and cook an additional 5 minutes. Remove filets from oil and drain. Serve immediately with 1/4 of butter mixture on each filet. Serves 4.

White Chocolate Almond Ice Cream

1 pint milk
1 pint cream
2 tablespoons vanilla
8 ounces white chocolate

8 eggs
8 ounces sugar
4 ounces toasted almonds,
  slivered

Combine milk, cream, vanilla and white chocolate in double boiler over boiling water. Heat until chocolate melts. Set aside to cool. Combine eggs and sugar in a separate bowl, whipping until ribbons form. Blend egg mixture with milk mixture. Stir in almonds and pour into ice cream freezer, freezing according to manufacturer's directions. Serves 8.

Hall's on the River

How many restaurants are so special that you remember wonderful evenings spent there twenty years ago? Hall's is that kind of place for a multitude of people. Those happy times with good friends and great food are frozen in your memory because Hall's is no ordinary restaurant. From fraternity groups to families, everyone feels it's "their place" to go when they have a special reason for dining out.

Hall's first opened almost twenty-five years ago serving juicy steaks and seafood. Their starter for every meal—a spicy, creamy cheese dip served with crackers—soon became famous. Everyone loved Hall's snappy beer cheese so much that they began to offer it in groceries all over the state. Today, Hall's menu still includes a beer cheese relish tray, beer cheese soup, fourteen other appetizers, and over thirty entrées. All dinners are served with a relish tray, rolls, hushpuppies, and your choice of two vegetables. For those of us watching our waistline, Hall's lists a whole section of lean and delicious dinners under the heading "Diet Center".

Last year, Hall's added a wonderful new deck that juts out over Howard's Creek. It proved enormously popular with regulars who prefer sitting out under the stars, listening to the sounds of water trickling slowly by and the wind playing through the trees. That's got to beat the sound of city traffic and the aroma of exhaust fumes, anytime!

Hall's offers an alternative way to dine, an altogether different way to spend an evening. Let me warn you, however—it may be addictive!

Owner: Howard's Creek Corporation
Address: 1225 Athens Boonesboro Road
         Winchester, Kentucky 40391
Telephone: (606) 255-8105
              (606) 527-6620
Hours & Day: Winter: Monday-Thursday 11:30 am to 9:00 pm
                Summer: Monday-Thursday 11:30 am to 10:00 pm
                Friday-Saturday 11:30 am to 11:00 pm
                Closed Sundays
Reservations accepted but not necessary
Visa, MasterCard, American Express
Directions: I-64 to exit 94 or 96, around Winchester, Highway 627 to
            Highway 418 (right turn).

     I-75 to exit 95, past Fort Boonesborough on Highway 418.

     Athens-Boonesboro Road (Highway 418) from Lexington.

LUNCHEON

Specialties

FOR A SANDWICH PLATTER ADD 1.75 TO PRICES BELOW.
ALL PLATTERS INCLUDE FRIES OR ONION RINGS AND HALL'S
HOMEMADE TANGY OR SWEET & CREAMY COLE SLAW.

Country Ham Sandwich	**3.95**
KENTUCKY CURED, OF COURSE, AND DELICIOUS	
Catfish Filet Sandwich	**3.95**
Hamburger	**2.50**
¼ POUND, FRESHLY GROUND, ON A SESAME BUN	
Cheeseburger	**2.75**
CHOOSE FROM CHEDDAR, SWISS, OR AMERICAN	
City Ham Sandwich	**2.50**
LEAN AND JUICY	
Ham & Swiss	**2.75**
TRY THIS COMBINATION ON LIGHT OR RYE BREAD	
Club	**3.95**
SELECT HAM OR TURKEY FOR THIS TOASTED TRIPLEDECKER	
Bacon, Lettuce and Tomato	**2.50**
HICKORY SMOKED BACON ON TOAST	
Lamb Fry Sandwich	**4.50**
OPEN-FACED, SMOTHERED IN CREAM GRAVY	
Barbeque Pork Sandwich	**3.75**
FRESHLY SLICED, MILDLY SPICED	
Hot Brown (luncheon portion)	**4.50**
A BLEND OF COUNTRY HAM, TURKEY AND CHEDDAR CHEESE SAUCE	
Grilled Cheese	**2.50**
CHEDDAR, SWISS, OR AMERICAN	

Special Of The Day

OUR CHEF PREPARES ONE OF HER FAVORITE DISHES EVERY DAY.
WE HOPE IT WILL BE ONE OF YOURS, TOO! . . . ASK YOUR SERVER

Halls Platters

ALL SERVED WITH FRIES, COLE SLAW & HUSHPUPPIES

Fried Clam Plate	**4.25**
GENEROUS PORTION OF CLAMS	
Fisherman's Platter	**4.95**
NOT REALLY A SANDWICH, BUT A FRESHWATER CATFISH FILET	
Fried Shrimp Platter	**5.25**
FIVE GOLDEN SHRIMP, FRIED TO GOLDEN BROWN IN OUR SPECIAL BATTER	

Companion Dishes

Rice Orleans	**1.25**
Vegetable of the Day	**1.25**
Buttered New Potatoes	**1.25**
Country Green Beans	**1.25**
Hall's Simply Terrific Onion Rings	**1.25**
SWEET BERMUDA ONIONS, FRIED IN OUR OWN BATTER	
Large Order of French Fries	**1.25**

Welcome —

Thank you for dining with us, please enjoy our delectable flavorings and quality foods. Hall's goes to great lengths to serve a wide variety of unique seafood and the choicest of specialties and steaks. We hope you will enjoy your meal as much as we enjoy having you with us.

— Hall's

APPETIZERS...
HOT

Potato Skins $4.50
Bacon, sour cream, green onion, loaded with cheddar cheese.

Hall's Original Fried Banana Peppers $2.95
We served 150,000 last year.

Zucchini $2.95
Served with Hall's hot sauce, ummm.

Veggie Combo $4.25
For those who can't decide…Peppers, Zucchini & Mushrooms.

Chicken Livers $3.95
Appetizer size with cream gravy.

Oyster Parks $5.95
One half-dozen select oysters wrapped in bacon and deep fried.

Fresh Fried Mushrooms $3.25
Never to be forgotten flavor.

Fried Clams $3.25
Sweet tender strips, lightly battered.

Chicken Fingers $4.25
Crispy tenderloin strips . . . honey mustard sauce.

Buffalo Wings $4.25
Spicy Creation . . . Special Sauce

NEW Beer Cheese Soup Bowl $2.50 Cup $1.60
Only Halls could create such a great soup. Good-N-Spicy

New England Seafood Chowder Bowl $2.50 Cup $1.60
Our traditional rich and creamy recipe made from scratch from fresh seafood and a special blend of spices.

COLD

Ocean Fresh Shrimp Cocktail $5.50
A longtime favorite—cool and light, topped with our special sauce.

Iced Steamed Shrimp 1/3 Lb. $6.50
Served U.P.S. (U-Peel Shrimp)

Spinach Salad $3.25
A delightful salad to compliment any dish, crisp bacon, fresh mushrooms, crumbled eggs and sprinkled with homemade croutons.

Fresh-Shucked Oysters 1/2 Doz. $5.95
Each $1.00
Flown in for you! Outstanding!

OR AS YOUR DINNER...

Shrimp Salad $7.50
Baby Shrimp, Eggs, Olives, Vegetables on a bed of fresh salad.

Hall's beer cheese …Absolutely Unmatched By Anyone!

BEER CHEESE RELISH TRAY	SMALL **3.75**
SERVED WITH CELERY, RADISHES & CRACKERS	LARGE **4.95**
CARRY OUT . . . . 5 OZ. **2.50**	8 OZ. **3.50**

HALL'S SPECIAL DRINKS

River Breeze
STARTS WITH VODKA…
AS COLD AS THE NAME IMPLIES.

Hawaiian Cooler
A SPECIAL RECIPE…
STARTING WITH LIGHT RUM.

Hall's Lemonade
A COOL, SWEET MIXTURE
OF LEMONS AND VODKA

ALL SERVED IN OUR HALLACIOUS GLASS $3.75

COLD N' CRISPY

House Salad $1.75
Diet Center Dressing & Crunchies

Spinach Salad $3.25
Mushrooms, Eggs, Diet Center Dressing & Crunchies

Ocean Fresh Shrimp Salad $7.50
Baby Gulf Shrimp, Egg Quarters, Ham Crunchies, on a bed of Lettuce.

HALL'S DIET CENTER DINNERS

All Our Entrees are served with Tossed House Salad, Diet Center Dressing, Crunchies, and Fresh Fruit.

Courtesy of Diet Center Winchester 744-0366
and Diet Center Lexington 252-THIN

Shrimply Delicious 5pc (4oz.) $8.50 8pc (8 oz.) $11.95
Plump Gulf Shrimp-Seasoned & Broiled

Fresh Flounder Filets 4oz. $6.95 8oz. $8.95
Extra lean, broiled just for you.

Grilled Chicken Breast 4oz. $6.95 8oz. $8.95
Boneless, skinless and broiled to perfection.

Halibut Steaks 4oz. $6.95 8oz. $8.95

ALL OF OUR DINNERS ARE SERVED WITH RELISH TRAY, ROLLS, HUSHPUPPIES, BUTTER, AND ANY TWO OF THE FOLLOWING:

French Fries	Pasta Salad	Vegetable of the Day
Onion Rings	Sweet and Creamy Cole Slaw	Green Beans
Baked Potato	Rice Orleans	New Potatoes
Fresh Tossed Salad	Hall's Original Tangy Slaw	Broccoli

——— HALL'S STANDS FOR HEALTH! ———
Everything at Hall's is homemade. We never use preservatives, additives or colorings. Hall's fries food in pure vegetable oils to give the best flavor to our products!

MARKET FRESH SEA FOOD

We stake our reputation on the quality and freshness of our seafood. We fly most seafood in from Boston, Baltimore, and New Orleans. Hall's recipes are carefully designed so that the full flavor of each item is particularly enhanced for your enjoyment. If there is any problem please ask for Hall's Manager!

Catch of the Day
A variety of seafood that has been flown in for you! Ask your Server what today's selections are . . .

Catfish $9.95
Hall's Specialty! You'll love these boneless filets.

Deviled Crab $9.75
3 — Seasoned for a taste tingling experience.

Fried Clam Dinner $9.95
A hearty serving of tender juicy clams.

Fresh Whole Catfish $9.50
Fried or broiled, approximately 14 oz. (Bone In)

Catfish & Frog Legs $12.50

Southern Seafood Combo $12.95
Catfish filet, frog legs, stuffed crabs & clams.

Oysters $12.95
Fresh, batter-dipped and golden brown.

Frog Legs $11.95
Tender white meat — fried or broiled.

Seafood for TWO $23.95
An exceptional quantity of catfish, frog legs, shrimp, and stuffed crabs.

Fried Shrimp Dinner $10.95
Plump shrimp, deep fried to a golden brown in our special batter. Crispy on the outside, tender and tasty on the inside.

Catfish & Shrimp $11.95

Snow Crab Legs
Please ask your Server about availability and price.

Fresh Sea Scallops Priced Daily
A generous serving that we will fry or broil.

Seafood Platter $14.95
Jumbo shrimp, catfish, scallops, oysters & deviled crab.

Orange Roughy Priced Daily
Seasweet, mild, filets . . . a favorite

Fresh Flounder Filets $10.95
Fried or broiled, you'll love it.

PRIME RIB
SEAFOOD, STEAK & RIB MARKET

Hall's uses only U.S.D.A. graded choice or better beef . . . and we prepare it to suit your discriminating taste.

Prime Rib of Beef Au Jus $12.95
Expertly seasoned to enhance the flavor, then slowly roasted to perfection.

Rib Eye 8 oz. $10.95
A juicy cut for smaller appetites, specially cut for those that enjoy the flavor of beef.

T-Bone $14.50
A full 14-oz. and charbroiled.

Strip Sirloin $13.95
10 oz. and sizzling with flavor.

Surf & Turf
A six oz. Rib Eye with 4 shrimp $12.95
or
6 oz. crab legs $13.95

Almaden House Wines
French Colombard, Rose, or Burgundy

Carafe 6.95   Half-Carafe 3.95   Glass 2.25

YOUR SERVER HAS HALLS FULL WINE LIST

PREMIUM WINE COOLERS $2.50

OUR FROSTED DRAFT BEER

MICHELOB
Miller Lite,

	12 OUNCE MUG	60 OUNCE PITCHER
	$1.25	$4.95

SPECIALTIES

Marinated Chicken Breast $9.95
Chargrilled to perfection.

Country Ham $9.95
Old Kentucky salt cured, with red eye gravy.

Boneless Breast of Chicken with Almond Pecan Stuffing $9.95
Served with creamy white wine & cheese sauce.

Lamb Fries $10.95
A platter full . . . . .truly different.

Kentucky River Hot Brown $9.95
A blend of country ham, turkey and Hall's own cheddar cheese sauce.

NEW Seafood Fettucini $9.95
Great Seafoods together with spinach fettucini in a classic sauce.

AND FINALLY...

Fresh Homemade Desserts of the Day Ask your server
Key Lime Pie $2.75
Hot Fudge Sundae $2.75
Cookies-n-Cream or Vanilla Ice Cream $1.50
Kentucky Mud Pie $2.75
Coffee Drinks $3.25

PSST...IF YOU'RE HAVING A BIRTHDAY OR ANNIVERSARY, TELL US — HALLS WOULD LOVE TO HELP YOU CELEBRATE IT!

Hall's is open all year

john conti. Gourmet Coffee
"The Best Coffee In Town"

On parties of 10 or more, we add on a gratuity of 15%, Thanks

Banana Peppers

1 large jar banana peppers,
  drained
1 cup milk
1/4 cup flour

1 1/4 pounds cracker meal,
  unseasoned
1 cup flour
1 1/4 tablespoons red pepper
Oil for deep frying

Cut peppers in half; soak in milk and flour. Combine cracker meal, flour, and red pepper to make breading mixture. Remove peppers from milk and roll in breading. Deep fry at 350 degrees until golden brown. Allow 3 peppers per person.

Hall's Beer Cheese

1 1/4 pounds sharp cheddar
  cheese
3/8 teaspoon garlic

1 cup flat beer
3/8 teaspoon red pepper

Mix all ingredients together until very smooth and creamy. Use as a dip for crackers, celery, or radishes.

Oysters Park

6 select oysters
6 slices bacon, halved
1 pound cracker meal

1 cup flour
3 cups milk
Oil for deep frying

Wrap each oyster with bacon and insert toothpick to hold securely. Mix cracker meal with flour. Dip wrapped oysters in milk; roll in flour and meal mixture. Deep fry at 350 degrees for 4 minutes or until golden brown. Yields 6.

Rice Orleans

1 cup rice
5 tablespoons margarine
 or butter
1 teaspoon garlic

1/4 cup Chablis or
 white cooking wine
1 green onion, chopped
2 cups mushrooms, sliced

Cook rice until tender. Set aside.

Melt margarine or butter; add garlic and wine. Sauté green onions and mushrooms until tender. Mix rice with sautéed mixture and heat.
Serves 4.

Catfish Filets

2 cups cornmeal
1 teaspoon salt
1/2 teaspoon red pepper
1 teaspoon black pepper

1 cup flour
1 pound catfish filets
Oil for deep frying

Mix meal, salt, peppers, and flour together. Roll catfish in this mixture until well coated. Deep fry catfish at 350 degrees for 3 to 4 minutes or until golden brown. Serves 2.

Kentucky Hot Brown

2 slices toast
3 ounces turkey
2 ounces country ham
2 slices of tomato

8 ounces white sauce*
2 ounces cheddar cheese
2 slices bacon

Cut 1 slice of toast diagonally. Place whole slice on bottom of hot brown plate or baking dish. Place 2 diagonal pieces on each side of whole toast. Layer turkey, ham, and tomato slices on top of toast. Pour warm white sauce over all. Cover hot brown with cheddar cheese; top with bacon. Bake at 350 degrees for 10 minutes. Serves 1.

*a roux of 6 tablespoons melted butter, 4 1/2 tablespoons flour, and 3 cups milk

Seafood Fettuccine

6 ounces whipping cream
1/2 teaspoon white pepper
1/2 teaspoon salt
1/2 teaspoon garlic
6 ounces egg noodles, cooked

6 ounces spinach fettuccine, cooked
3 ounces shrimp
3 ounces crabmeat
Parmesan cheese

Combine cream, pepper, salt, and garlic; bring to a slow boil. Add noodles and fettuccine. Add shrimp and crabmeat. Mix well, sprinkle with Parmesan cheese and serve hot. Serves 2.

Kentucky River Mud Pie

1 9-inch graham cracker crust
Chocolate syrup
Coffee ice cream

Slivered almonds
Whipped topping

Drizzle pie crust with syrup; fill with ice cream. Drizzle syrup over ice cream. Sprinkle with almonds and freeze. Serve frozen with whipped topping, additional syrup, and almonds. Serves 6.

Hyatt

The Hyatt Regency in Lexington is a constant hub of activity. There always seems to be a basketball game, a concert, a prom, a convention, or a party in progress, spilling out into the Hyatt, creating a fun and festive atmosphere. Yet the Hyatt's two wonderful restaurants consistently offer great food and great service in a quiet, relaxed atmosphere.

Perhaps it's the cascading fountain in The Glass Garden that soothes and calms. The wonderful outdoor atmosphere is a backdrop for breakfast, lunch, and dinner. An eclectic menu offers regional favorites such as catfish, fried chicken, steak, and specialties from Italian to Chinese. The Sunday brunch is outstanding. Fabulous decorations and a lengthy and lavish buffet transforms the restaurant into a feast for the eyes and the palate.

Downstairs, The Grill at 400 West offers a new and creative approach to dining called "rock cuisine". This trend utilizes blocks of Swiss granite heated to over 500 degrees and brought tableside so patrons may do the cooking. This is not only a healthy way to prepare seafood, chops, steaks, and vegetables, but makes for a fun way to spend the evening. Any favorite menu item can be prepared by the chefs, too - grilled to perfection and served piping hot with baked potatoes, fresh vegetables, and great breads. The flexible menu offers new items on a daily basis, always fresh and always good.

While the Hyatt is certainly fun and festive, it also offers a lovely and relaxed place to dine, whatever your taste.

Glass Garden
Owners: Hyatt Regency Lexington
Address: 400 West Vine
      Lexington, Kentucky 40507
Telephone: (606) 253-1234
Hours & Days: Sunday-Saturday 6:00 am to 11:00 pm
Reservations not required
All major credit cards accepted
Directons: Downtown Lexington in the Hyatt Regency.
      Enter at the mall or second level.

The Grill at 400 West
Owners: Hyatt Regency Lexington
      400 West Vine
      Lexington, Kentucky 40507
Telephone: (606) 253-4745
Hours & Days: Monday-Thursday 6:00 pm to 11:00 pm
      Friday-Saturday 6:00 pm to 11:30 am
      Sunday 5:00 pm to 10:00 pm
Reservations recommended
All major credit cards accepted
Directions: Downtown Lexington in the Hyatt Regency.
      Enter off the lobby.

Glass Garden

Sandwiches/Burgers

CREATE YOUR OWN 6.25
From the Deli with Your Choice of Corned Beef, Turkey, Ham, Roast Beef, Swiss or Cheddar Cheese, Served on Sunflower Wheat Bread

TUNA MELT 6.25
Tuna Salad on an English Muffin with Sliced Tomatoes and Glazed with Provolone Cheese

STEAK SANDWICH 8.95
Rib Eye Steak on Viennese Style Bread with Lettuce and Tomato

REUBEN'S REUBEN 6.25
Thinly Sliced New York Corned Beef, Glazed with Gruyere Cheese, Served Open Faced on Rye Bread with Sauerkraut and a Kosher Pickle Spear

YOUR BASIC BURGER 5.95
8 oz. Fresh Beef Burger with Lettuce, Tomato, Red Onion and Steak Fries, on a Sesame Seed Bun

VERMONT BURGER 6.75
We Add Vermont Cheddar Cheese Melted Over Lean, Crisp Bacon Strips

CHARLIE CHAN'S CHICKEN 7.25
Charbroiled Breast of Chicken, Marinated in Teriyaki Sauce and Pineapple Juice, Served with Lettuce on a Sesame Seed Bun with Steak Fries

SEAWICH 7.50
Char-Grilled Fresh Fish Filet on a Kaiser Roll with Tomato, Iceburg Lettuce, Olive Oil, White Wine Vinegar and Herbs

Appetizers

CARIBBEAN SCALLOPS 6.50
Blackened Scallops Atop a Bed of Caribbean Spiced Linguine with Pine Nuts

TORTELLINI 4.95
Hand Rolled Egg and Spinach Pasta Filled with Cheese and Veal, Served in a Creamy Sauce

FROM THE GULF 6.95
Five Juicy Jumbo Gulf Shrimp, Served with Cocktail Sauce

SKINS 'N' THINGS 3.95
Potato Skins Deep-Fried, Topped with Bits of Bacon, Melted Cheddar Cheese, Green Onions and Sour Cream

NACHOS SUPREME 3.75
Corn Tortillas, Topped with Refried Beans, Guacamole, Pico De Gallo, Melted Cheddar and Sour Cream, Served with Salsa and Jalapenos

MOZZARELLA STICKS 3.95
Deep-Fried to Perfection, Accompanied By Marinara Sauce

PURELY POULTRY 4.00
Fried Chicken Strips, Served with Honey Mustard Sauce

MARKET SALAD 3.25
Crisp Greens, Ripe Beefsteak Tomatoes, Bermuda Onions, Virgin Olive Oil and Balsalmic Vinegar Dressing

Salads et al

TACO SALAD 6.95
Crisp Tortilla Shell with Chili, Lettuce, Sour Cream, Guacamole, Tomato, Olives and Jalapenos

CHICKEN IN THE FIELD 7.25
Lightly Breaded and Boned Breast with Fresh Field Greens and Cabernet Vinaigrette Dressing

COBB SALAD 5.95
Romaine Lettuce, Avocado, Chicken, Bleu Cheese, Tomato and Bacon, Served with an Oil and Vinegar Dressing

PASTA 5.25
Wagon Wheel Pasta with Tomato, Basil, Olive Oil, Onions, Capers and Almonds

FRESH FRUIT PALETTE 5.50
A Medley of Sliced Fresh Seasonal Fruit Served with a Freshly Baked Muffin and Yogurt

EGGS ANY TIME 5.95
Served Any Way with Bacon, Ham or Sausage, Fresh Bakeries and Fruit Garnish or a Fluffy Three Egg Omelette with Your Choice of Cheese, Bell Peppers, Mushrooms and Ham

COUNTRY HAM AND FRIED EGG 5.95
Center Cut Country Ham Steak, Fried Egg with Lettuce, Tomato, Mayonnaise on Farm House Bread

Bluegrass Specials

HOT BROWN 7.25
Fine Grain Bread Piled High with Sliced Breast of Turkey and Smothered in a Satin Cheese Sauce and Crowned with Bacon Strips, Tomato and Sprinkled with Grated Parmesan Cheese

SOUTHERN FRIED CHICKEN 8.95
Seasoned Chicken Pieces Cooked 'til Golden Brown By the Chef

DEEP-FRIED CATFISH 8.25
Tender Filets of Catfish, Served with Fresh Vegetables and French Fried Potatoes

Featured Entrees

All the Entrees Listed Below Include a Garden Salad

SHRIMP AND BEEF 15.50
Four Butterflied Jumbo Shrimp, a 4 oz. Filet of Beef Grilled and Served with a Lemon Pepper Sauce

FAJITAS . . . OUR WAY 11.95
A Sizzling Skillet, Filled with Spicy Beef, Chicken or Shrimp, or a Combo. Served with a Stack of Tortillas, Guacamole, Sour Cream and Pico de Gallo

ORIGINAL STIR FRY 14.25
Fresh Shrimp and Scallops, Stir Fried with Oriental Style Vegetables, Water Chestnuts and Fried Rice

FRESH FISH
We Serve Only Fresh Fish Which Often Includes, Depending on Seasonal Availability, GROUPER, MAHI-MAHI, RED FISH, SALMON, SHARK, SNAPPER, SWORDFISH or TROUT Prepared Broiled, Sauteed, Steamed or Blackened Cajun Style.
Market Price

LINGUINE 12.75
With Clams, Garlic, Parsley, Tomatoes, Virgin Olive Oil, White Wine, Romano Cheese and Garlic Bread

HICKORY SMOKED SPARE RIBS 12.75
All You Can Eat! Hickory Smoked Spare Ribs. Served with Cole Slaw and Steak Fries

STEAKS
Cut From 14 Day Aged Beef, Served with Angel Hair Onions, Baked Potato and Bearnaise Sauce
Rib Eye 8 oz. 12.00   Filet 8 oz. 13.75

For that special balance between taste, nutrition and low calories, Hyatt Hotels is proud to present . . .

Perfect Balance®

ORIENTAL STEAMED BASKET WITH VEGETABLES AND FISH 8.75
Fresh Seasonal Fish Steamed with Tender Vegetables. Presented in an Oriental Steamer.
Approximately: Calories 183, Carbohydrates (grams) 14, Fat (grams) 2, Cholesterol (grams) .05, Sodium (grams) .1, Protein (grams) 29

VEGETARIAN LASAGNE 6.75
Whole Wheat Pasta Layered with Fresh Vegetables and Light Cheese, Baked in a Basil Flavored Tomato Sauce.
Approximately: Calories 485, Carbohydrates (grams) 40, Fat (grams) 44, Cholesterol (grams) .03, Sodium (grams) .9, Protein (grams) 25

CHICKEN BREAST WITH RED PEPPER SAUCE 7.50
Sliced Breast of Chicken Garnished with Steamed Spinach, Sweet Red Pepper Sauce, Julienne Peppers and Toasted Pignolias Nuts.
Approximately: Calories 322, Carbohydrates (grams) 17, Fat (grams) 18, Cholesterol (grams) .1, Sodium (grams) 6, Protein (grams) 41

Soup, Salad and Dessert Bar

5.95

AS AN ACCOMPANIMENT WITH ANY MEAL
3.95

Displayed on the Bar is a Chef's Kettle with a Freshly Made Soup and an Array of Colorful Salads Which Combine a Variety of Fresh and Imaginative Ingredients and Desserts, Including Frozen Yogurt

SOUP OF THE DAY
Cup 1.75   Bowl 2.50

BEAN SOUP
Cup 1.75   Bowl 2.50

Fruit of the Vine

We Offer the Following Selection of Fine Wine By the Glass

CHARDONNAY 3.50
Chateau Ste. Michelle, Washington State

FUME BLANC 3.00
J. Lohr, California

WHITE BURGUNDY 3.75
Macon Blanc, Louis Jadot

WHITE ZINFANDEL 3.50
Bel Arbres, Redwood Valley

GAMAY 3.00
J. Lohr, California

RED BURGUNDY 3.75
Beaujolais Villages, Louis Jadot

SPARKLING WHITE 3.75
Domaine Chandon Hyatt Cuvee, California

STARTERS

Cold   Prawn Cocktail $5.50
Chilled Grilled Vegetables with Avocado Sauce $4.50
Mussels and Oysters Combo with Pepper and Vinaigrette $4.75

Hot   Chef's BBQ Ribs $4.50
Fried Shrimp $6.95
Banana Peppers with Spicy Jack Cheese $3.95
Onion Gold Brick $3.95
Fried Artichoke Hearts $3.95
The Grill Onion Soup $2.75

——————— ROCK CUISINE ———————

We provide the hot rock, natural granite from the Swiss Alps, and the raw
ingredients of your choice. You then use the hot rock, which is heated
to 500°, to grill your entree to your liking.
Our Grill Salad and a Baked Potato are included with all Rock Cuisine Entrees.

BREAST OF CHICKEN $9.95
with Sweet Teriyaki, Spicy Cajun and Lemon-Garlic Sauce

SIRLOIN OF BEEF $11.95
with Bearnaise and Horseradish Sauces

GULF SHRIMP AND SCALLOPS $12.95
with Teriyaki and Bum Sauces together with Drawn Butter

VEGETABLES $8.95
Italian Style with Marinara and Jerk Sauces

COMBINATION - SWORDFISH, SALMON and GROUPER $12.95
with Bum and Teriyaki Sauces

COMBINATION - CHICKEN - BEEF - SHRIMP $12.95
with Bearnaise, Teriyaki and Jerk Sauces

* * * * * * * * * * FROM THE GRILL * * * * * * * * * * *

NEW ZEALAND LOBSTER TAIL AND FILET $16.95

With our Prime Dry Aged Beef - and Freshest Seafood.
Steaks and Chops may be ordered with garlic and/or grilled
Onions and Mushrooms.

Our Grill Salad and your choice of Wild Rice, Baked Potato or Pasta are
included with all Grill Entrees.

PORTERHOUSE
24 Ounce $17.00   48 Ounce, for Two $30.00

STEAKS AND CHOPS

New York 8 Ounce $10.95	Filet 8 Ounce $10.95	
12 Ounce $14.50	12 Ounce $14.50	

LONDON BROIL $11.95
12 Ounce Marinated Steak

RIBEYE $12.50
12 Ounce, Topped with Pesto

LAMB CHOPS $14.95
Lightly Breaded with Dijon
Mustard Sauce

CHICKEN $9.95
Stuffed with Mushrooms, Dried
Tomatoes, Basil Sauce

ROASTED DUCK $13.95
with Amaretto Sauce

FRESH SEAFOOD
Blackened, Grilled, Sauteed or Broiled

FILET OF SALMON $11.95   SCALLOPS SCAMPI $11.95
SWORDFISH STEAK $13.95   GROUPER $11.95

EXPRESSO and CAPPUCINO Available

*Childrens Portion - 1/2 Portion for 1/2 the Price

Fried Artichokes

6 artichoke hearts
1/2 cup flour
1/2 cup cornmeal
Salt and pepper to taste
2 whole eggs
Milk
2 cups bread crumbs

1/2 teaspoon cayenne pepper
1 teaspoon basil
1 teaspoon oregano
1 teaspoon thyme
1 1/2 teaspoons seasoned salt
Chili Mayonnaise*

Cut artichoke hearts in half. Combine flour and cornmeal with salt and pepper. Roll hearts in seasoned flour. Beat eggs slightly, add enough milk for dipping. Season bread crumbs with cayenne pepper, basil, oregano, thyme and seasoned salt. Dip hearts in egg and milk mixture, then roll in bread crumbs. Fry until golden brown. Serve with chili mayonnaise. Serves 2.

Chili Mayonnaise:
1 cup mayonnaise
1/2 teaspoon cayenne pepper
1 tablespoon chili powder
2 teaspoons Worcestershire sauce

Mix all ingredients together.

Mussels Provençal

6 to 7 medium mussels
1 tablespoon olive oil
2 teaspoons garlic
3 tablespoons fresh tomato, diced
3 tablespoons potato, peeled and diced

2 tablespoons white wine
1 tablespoon lemon juice
2 tablespoons mussel juice
2 tablespoons butter, softened
1 tablespoon parsley, chopped
1/2 tablespoon basil, chopped
Salt and pepper to taste

Pre-steam mussels. Open and cut mussel loose. Keep 1/2 shell only. In sauce pan, add olive oil and sauté garlic, tomato, and potato for 2 to 3 minutes. Deglaze with white wine, reduce, add lemon and mussel juices, and reduce again. Remove from heat and incorporate soft butter, parsley and basil. Check seasonings and pour on top of all mussel shells. Serves 1.

Char Broiled Shrimp Salad

3 large shrimp
2 ounces Cajun sauce (available in grocery stores)
1/2 radicchio
2 leaves Romaine lettuce

1 leaf Belgium endive
4 leaves spinach
1/4 fresh tomato
1 lemon wedge
Ranch dressing

Peel and devein shrimp. Marinate in Cajun sauce for 1 hour. Arrange radicchio, Romaine lettuce, Belgium endive, and spinach leaves on plate. Char broil shrimp and place on greens. Garnish with tomato and lemon. Serve ranch dressing on the side. Serves 1.

Cobb Salad

5 ounces iceberg lettuce
1/2 white of one hard-boiled egg
1 ounce fresh tomato, diced
2 ounces chicken breast,
   cooked, skinned
1/2 avocado

1 tablespoon bacon bits
1 tablespoon bleu cheese,
   crumbled
1 leek, sliced lengthwise
Salad dressing of your choice

Place cut iceberg lettuce in center of plate. Julienne or dice the next 4 items. Place all ingredients in individual sections on lettuce. Sprinkle with bacon bits and bleu cheese crumbles. Serve with dressing of your choice. Garnish with sliced leeks. Serves 1.

Scallops Scampi

2 tablespoons olive oil
1 teaspoon garlic, minced
4 ounces fresh sea scallops
2 pieces large shrimp
2 ounces white wine

1/2 cup heavy cream
1/4 cup tomato, chopped
2 tablespoons fresh basil
Pasta
2 green onions, diced

Heat olive oil and sauté garlic, scallops and shrimp. Deglaze with white wine. Add heavy cream, reduce, and add tomato and fresh basil. Serve over pasta. Garnish with green onions. Serves 1.

Seafood Brochette

2 ounces salmon
2 ounces swordfish
2 ounces tuna
1 green onion

1 red pepper
1/2 head radicchio
Marinade*

Scallop fish. Using 2 bamboo skewers, spear salmon, pepper, swordfish, tuna, onion, and radicchio. Brush with marinade and cook under the broiler for 2 to 3 minutes. Finish on the grill. (Grill radicchio separately from seafood brochette.) Any type of firm fish, shrimp, or scallop can be substituted. Serves 1.

*Marinade:
1/2 cup olive oil
1 tablespoon garlic, chopped
1 tablespoon fresh thyme,
   chopped

1 tablespoon rosemary, chopped
1 tablespoon fresh lemon juice

Mix all ingredients together.

Glass Garden Cheesecake

1 7/8 pounds cream cheese
2 cups sugar
3 tablespoons cornstarch
2 cups sour cream

5 eggs
2 1/4 teaspoons vanilla
1/4 teaspoon salt
1 graham cracker crust

Whip cream cheese, sugar and cornstarch until smooth. Scrape bowl, add sour cream, and mix. Add eggs one at a time. Incorporate vanilla and salt. Line a 9x12 pan with graham crackers. Add mix and bake in a water bath at 325 degrees until firm, 50 to 60 minutes. Don't overbake. Let cool at least two hours. Serves 12.

Tira Mi Su

1 pound 2 ounces Mascarpone*
3 cups heavy cream
1 1/2 cups superfine sugar
3 tablespoons Kahlua

1/2 teaspoon coffee paste**
1 teaspoon vanilla
1/2 cup cocoa powder
2 10-inch chocolate cakes

Whip Mascarpone until smooth. Add cream and sugar slowly. Add Kahlua and coffee paste, blend until smooth and add vanilla. Spread half of mix on top of one cake and smooth to 1/2 inch thick. Do not ice sides. Dust with cocoa powder. Repeat procedure for remaining cake. Makes 2 single layer cakes.

*A soft cheese available in cheese shops.

**Available in fine coffee shops or can be made by mixing a strong, thick paste of instant coffee, water, butter and pastry flour.

Joe Bologna's

J oe Bologna's Italian Restaurant is beloved by everyone. Kids love it because they serve the best pizza in the world, students love it because it's a really happening place, business people love the handy location, families love the friendliness, and they all love the absolutely wonderful food!

Joe and Anne Bologna have been creating edible Italian masterpieces for years, and only recently have moved into a much-needed roomier location. In a stroke of genius, the Bologna's realized the historic church across the street would be perfect for their restaurant. A beautiful renovation took place, and—without missing a beat—the luscious aroma of homemade marinara sauce began wafting from Lexington's first church restaurant. Built in 1890 as the Maxwell Street Presbyterian Church, and sold in 1914 to the Orthodox Synagogue, the original stained glass windows are still in place. A new loft was added upstairs for parties of up to fifty.

It is a pleasure just listening to Anne Bologna talk about their recipes and their food. "Our marinara sauce bubbles all day long in huge pots." When asked about the Vegetable Pasta Salad, Ann explains that "We make that more in the summer when fresh basil is available for the pesto sauce." Only the freshest ingredients are used. Everything is homemade, and a touch of love and care go in at no extra charge.

Joe Bologna's popularity is no accident. This truly is a friendly, social gathering place, that serves affordable, fabulous Italian food in a highly-convenient area of town. You can't ask for more than that!

Owners: Anne and Joe Bologna
Address: 120 West Maxwell Street
         Lexington, Kentucky 40508
Telephone: (606) 252-4933
Hours & Days: Monday-Thursday 11:00 am to midnight
         Friday-Saturday 11:00 am to 1:00 am
         Sunday 12:00 noon to 11:00 pm
         Closed New Year's Day, Easter, Thanksgiving, Christmas
Reservations not required
Visa, MasterCard
Directions: 2 blocks from downtown Lexington.
         South Broadway to West Maxwell.

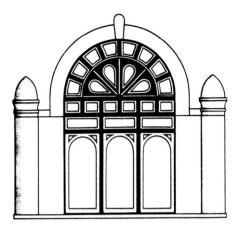

JOE BOLOGNA'S

APPETIZERS

Sautéed Mushrooms In Burgundy And
Butter Sauce 3.50

Fried Hot Banana Peppers 2.95

Fried Zucchini 2.95

Fried Mushrooms 3.25

Fried Mozzarella Cheese Sticks 3.95

Fried Appetizer Combination - A Sampling
Of Cheese Sticks, Zucchini, Mushrooms,
And Banana Peppers 3.50

Zucchini Parmesan Or Eggplant Parmesan 3.95

*Fried Appetizers Served With Horseradish
Or Marinara Sauce*

SIDE ORDERS

One Garlic Breadstick .70 (Joe's Specialty)

Seasoned Potato Wedges 1.25

Onion Rings 2.25

Seasoned Potato Wedges/Onion Rings Combo 1.75

Spaghetti With Marinara Or Meat Sauce 3.50

Homemade Soup 1.95

Chili (In Season) 2.50

Cream Soup Of The Day (In Season) 2.75

BEVERAGES

Soft Drinks .95
Pepsi, Diet Pepsi, 7-Up, Mt. Dew, Dr. Pepper

Fresh Iced Tea .75   Hot Tea .75

Milk 1.00

Coffee - Regular Or Decaffeinated .75

SEE OUR BEER & WINE MENU

SALADS

Dressings: House Italian, Ranch, French, Bacon,
Thousand Island, Bleu Cheese, Oil & Vinegar
Extra Dressing .25

Tossed Salad - With Tomatoes, Black Olives,
Sliced Cucumber, Pepperoncini And Croutons 2.50

Chef Salad - A Bed Of Fresh Salad Topped With
Sliced Cucumbers, Tomatoes, Black Olives,
Pepperoncini, Red Onions, Egg Slices And A Choice
Of Any Three Of The Following Items:

Swiss, Provolone, American, Fontinella Cheese,
Ham, Bacon, Turkey, Salami,
Asparagus, Mushrooms, Anchovies
Chef Salad Served With One Breadstick 5.25

Antipasto - A Bed Of Fresh Salad Topped With
Cucumber Slices, Tomatoes, Black Olives,
Pepperoncini, Mushrooms, Artichokes, Salami,
Pepperoni, Anchovy, Capicola Ham, Fontinella And
Provolone Cheese Served With House Italian Dressing
For One 3.25   For Two 5.75

Spinach Salad - Fresh, Crisp Spinach Topped With
Mushrooms, Egg Slices, Red Onions, Bacon Crumbles
And Hot Bacon Dressing 3.50

Chicken Pasta Salad - Chilled Ziti And Chicken
With Almonds, Celery, Green Peppers, Sweet Relish
And Pimento In A Special Dressing Arranged On A
Bed Of Lettuce Garnished With Tomato Wedges And
Black Olives 3.95

Vegetable Pasta Salad - Fresh Broccoli, Carrots,
And Zucchini With Onions, Peas, Pimento And Chilled
Pasta Shells In Our Homemade Pesto Sauce On A Bed
Of Lettuce 3.95 (Summer Special)

ROUND PIZZA

SERVES	1	2-3	4-6
	8"	12"	16"
Cheese	4.00	7.50	12.50
One Item	4.60	8.50	14.25
Two Items	5.10	9.25	16.00
Three Items	5.50	10.00	17.75
Four Items	5.95	11.00	19.50
All Vegetable	5.95	11.00	19.50

(Green & Hot Peppers, Green And Black Olives,
Onions, Muchrooms)

Everything	(Unavailable)	12.95	21.95
Extra Cheese	.25	.50	.85
Extra Sauce	.15	.20	.25
Extra Item	(Unavailable)	.70	.90

SICILIAN PAN PIZZA

SERVES	2-3	3-4	4-6
	8x10	10x14	12x17
Cheese	5.70	9.25	12.50
One Item	6.60	10.50	14.25
Two Items	7.50	11.70	16.00
Three Items	8.40	12.90	17.75
Four Items	9.30	13.95	19.50
All Vegetable	9.30	13.95	19.50

(Green & Hot Peppers, Green And Black Olives,
Onions, Mushrooms)

Everything	10.95	16.95	21.95
Extra Cheese	.50	.85	.95
Extra Sauce	.20	.25	.35
Extra Item	.70	.90	1.10

PIZZA ITEMS

Ham, Bacon, Pepperoni, Sausage, Hamburger, Anchovy, Pineapple,
Onions, Mushrooms, Black Olives, Green Olives, Hot Peppers, Green Peppers

SPECIALTY PIZZA

MEATBALL -
Meatballs Top Mounds Of
Mozzarella Cheese, Marinara Sauce
and Crushed Red Pepper

HAWAIIAN - Ham, Green
Peppers And Pineapple Top
Mild Barbecue Sauce And
Mozzarella Cheese

	8"	12"	16"
Meatball	4.85	9.25	14.75
Sfingione	6.00	10.95	16.95
Hawaiian	6.00	10.95	16.95
Mexican	6.70	13.75	19.95

(Only Round Pizza Available)

SFINGIONE - Sautéed
Onions With Anchovies, Tomatoes
Mozzarella & Romano Cheeses

MEXICAN - Seasoned
Ground Beef, Cheddar Cheese,
Jalepeño And Green Peppers,
Onions, Black Olives, Tomatoes.
Served With A Side Dish Of Sour
Cream

—DINING ROOM AND CARRYOUT OPEN SEVEN DAYS A WEEK—

DINNERS

Joe Bologna's is proud to offer a wide selection of homemade pasta dinners and other Italian specialities - something for every taste!
All Dinners Served With One Garlic Breadstick
And Your Choice Of Soup Or Tossed Salad
Spinach Salad May Replace Either Of The Above Choices For $1.50 Extra
Dressings - House Italian, Ranch, French, Bacon, Thousand Island, Bleu Cheese, Oil & Vinegar

HOMEMADE SPECIALTIES

Lasagne - An Italian Classic Created With Lean Beef And Pork, Authentic Ricotta Cheese And Spices - All Layered Between Lasagne Noodles And Covered With Homemade Marinara Sauce
          Small 7.50   Large 8.50

Vegetable Lasagne - A Real Favorite! Fresh Broccoli And Zucchini Replace The Meat For A Truly Unique Dish
          Small 7.50   Large 8.50

Cannelloni - Pasta Stuffed With Spinach, Ground Round And Covered With Homemade Marinara Sauce
          Small 7.50   Large 8.95

Manicotti - A Ricotta Cheese Filled Pasta Shell Topped With Homemade Marinara Sauce
          Small 7.50   Large 8.95

Mostaccioli - Small Tube-Shaped Pasta Covered With Homemade Meat Sauce
          Small 6.50   Large 7.95

Linguine - Pasta With Red Clam Sauce
          8.95

Linguine - Pasta With White Clam Sauce
          8.95

Gift Certificates & Joe B. T-Shirts Available

FETTUCCINE

Thin Pasta "Ribbons" With A Choice Of Sauce

	Small	Large
With Butter Sauce	6.95	8.65
With Homemade Marinara Sauce	7.25	8.75
With Homemade Meat Sauce	7.50	8.95
Alfredo Sauce - Butter, Cream And Parmesan Cheese	7.95	9.25
Alfredo Sauce With Ham, Bacon, And Green Pepper	8.50	9.95

SPAGHETTI

	Small	Large
With Homemade Marinara Sauce	5.50	6.25
With Homemade Meat Sauce	6.50	7.95
With Meatballs & Homemade Meat Sauce	7.50	8.95
With Italian Sausage & Meat Sauce	7.50	8.95
Zucchini Parmesan With Spaghetti	6.50	7.95
Eggplant Parmesan With Spaghetti	6.50	7.95

DESSERT

Single Scoop—Vanilla 1.25
Hot Fudge Sundae   2.50
PARFAITS 3.00   Creme de Menthe
          Toasted Almond - Amaretto/Kahlúa
Kahlúa   Creme de Menthe/Hot Fudge

Cheesecake Of The Day - Ask Your Server 2.00

SUBMARINES & SANDWICHES

One-Fourth Pound Hamburger
100% Beef With Lettuce, Tomato, Onion And Mayonnaise - A Traditional Favorite.   3.95
Bacon .50 extra

One-Third Pound Italian Hamburger
A Joe B. Original - Lightly Spiced With Italian Seasoning, Topped With Lettuce, Tomato, Red Onion And Mayonnaise.   4.95

Grilled Cheese   1.95

Bacon, Lettuce & Tomato   2.25

Meatball Sub - Sliced Meatballs Topped With Homemade Marinara Sauce
          Half 3.25   Whole 5.75

Eggplant Or Zucchini Parmesan Sub - A Great Treat For The Vegetarian! Deep-fried Eggplant Or Zucchini Slices Topped With Marinara Sauce And Mozzarella Cheese
          Half 2.95   Whole 4.95

Capicola Ham And Swiss Cheese Sub - Spicy Ham With Imported Swiss Cheese, Lettuce, Tomato And Special Dressing
          Half 3.25   Whole 5.75

Sausage Sub - Spicy Links Of Italian Sausage With **Choice** Of Sautéed Onions And Green Peppers **Or** Marinara Sauce, Onions And Green Peppers
          Half 3.25   Whole 5.75

Cheese, Hot Peppers Or Additional Items
$.40 Extra
Half Sub Items $.20 Extra

All Sandwiches Are Served
With Seasoned Potato Wedges And A Pickle

Beef, Turkey, Bacon Club • A Hearty Sandwich
For That Big Appetite! Served With Lettuce, Tomato And Mayonnaise - Wheat Or White Bread.   5.50

Salami And Provolone Sub - Authentic Genoa Salami And Provolone Cheese, Lettuce, Tomato, And Dijon Mustard - **Served Hot or Cold**
          Half 2.95   Whole 4.95

Beef Sub - Mounds Of Roast Beef Grilled With Onion, Green Peppers And Cheese With Our Own Special Sauce
          Half 2.95   Whole 4.95

Ham Sub - Grilled Lean Sliced Ham Topped With Lettuce, Tomato, Mayonnaise And Dijon Mustard
          Half 2.95   Whole 4.95

Italian Sub - A Great Combination Of Capicola Ham, Salami, Pepperoni, Mortadella, Provolone Cheese, Lettuce, Tomato, Onion And House Italian Dressing - **Served Hot or Cold**
          Half 3.95   Whole 5.95

Joe B's Stromboli - Sausage And Ground Beef Patty Topped With Pizza Sauce, Grilled Onions, Green Peppers And Provolone Cheese
          Half 3.35   Whole 5.95

Submarine Buns Are Toasted

Chicken Pasta Salad

2 pounds cooked chicken, diced
6 ounces celery, chopped
4 ounces green pepper, chopped
2 pimientos, finely chopped
Salt and pepper to taste

1 pound ziti pasta,
   cooked in salt water, drained
1 cup toasted almonds
Pasta Dressing*
   (or Thousand Island Dressing)

Mix chicken and vegetables together; season with salt and pepper. Fold in pasta. Place mixture on salad plates, sprinkle with almonds and top with dressing. Serves 6 to 8.

*Pasta Dressing:
1 cup French dressing

2 cups mayonnaise
3/4 cup sweet relish

Mix ingredients together and refrigerate. Makes approximately 3 cups.

Vegetable Pasta Salad

4 ounces carrots, thinly sliced
2 ounces small broccoli florets
2 ounces small cauliflower
   florets
1 6-ounce zucchini,
   sliced 1/4-inch and quartered

6 ounces onions,
   diced 1/4 to 1/2-inch
1 pimiento, finely chopped
3/4 cup frozen peas
1/2 pound medium pasta shells,
   cooked and drained
1 cup Pesto Sauce*

Cook all vegetables in boiling water until tender, but still firm. Place pasta on plate, cover with vegetables, and top with Pesto Sauce. Serves 8 to 10.

*Pesto Sauce:
1 1/2 cups basil, loosely packed
1 1/2 cups parsley,
   loosely packed
1 1/2 cups olive oil
5 cloves fresh garlic

1/2 cup walnuts
3/4 cup Romano cheese
1 teaspoon salt

Place all ingredients in blender and blend on high speed. Heat and serve over pasta and vegetables.

Chicken Pasta Primavera

1 cup broccoli, chopped
1/3 cup onion, chopped
2 cloves garlic, finely chopped
1 carrot, cut into thin strips
3 tablespoons olive oil
2 cups cooked chicken, diced
1 teaspoon salt

2 medium tomatoes, chopped
4 cups hot macaroni shells,
  or cooked linguine
Marinara sauce, optional
1/3 cup Parmesan cheese,
  grated
Snipped parsley

Cook broccoli, onion, garlic and carrot in olive oil over medium heat until broccoli is crisp-tender, approximately 10 minutes. Stir in chicken, salt and tomatoes; heat 5 minutes. Add 1 small ladle of Marinara sauce, if desired. Spoon chicken mixture over prepared pasta; sprinkle with Parmesan cheese and parsley. Serves 6.

Fettuccine Alfredo

5 ounces fresh fettuccine
3/4 ounce butter
1/2 tablespoon parsley,
  finely chopped

2 ounces heavy cream
1 1/4 teaspoons Parmesan cheese
1/2 dash white pepper
1/2 dash salt

Heat fettuccine in a strainer in hot water for 10 seconds. Remove; shake strainer until water is thoroughly drained from fettuccine.

Melt butter until bubbly and add parsley. When mixture is again bubbly, add cream and simmer 1 minute. Add cheese, salt and pepper. Simmer 90 seconds, until sauce starts to thicken. Toss with fettuccine and serve. Serves 1.

Entrée

Linguine with White Clam Sauce

2 cloves fresh garlic, chopped
5 tablespoons olive oil
3 teaspoons parsley, chopped
1 6.5-ounce can clams,
  with liquid

6 dashes pepper
4 dashes oregano
8 ounces linguine,
  freshly cooked

For sauce: sauté garlic in olive oil for 2 minutes. Stir in parsley and sauté 1 minute more. Add liquid from clams and simmer 2 minutes. Add clams, pepper, and oregano; simmer an additional 2 minutes.

Heat linguine in strainer in hot water for 10 seconds. Shake strainer of linguine to drain thoroughly. Serve clam sauce over linguine. Serves 1.

L&N Seafood Grill

Located in the fashionable Lexington Green Mall on Nicholasville Road, L&N Seafood Grill stands out as a symbol of excellence and innovation. They serve the freshest of seafoods in wonderfully delicious ways.

With lots of windows, brass, green plants, exposed brick, and dark green walls, the atmosphere is friendly and comfortable. There is a wonderful patio outside that overlooks a small lake. Here, weather permitting, hungry crowds may choose to dine while enjoying a beautiful view.

The menu is a celebration of traditional seafood cookery, offering something for absolutely everyone. L&N Seafood offers broiled, fried, creole or cajun style, and their house specialty is grilled over mesquite wood charcoal. Just as all their fish is fresh, their biscuits, sauces, salads, and desserts are all made from scratch and each entrée is prepared to order. Everyone loves these hot, fluffy, slightly sweet biscuits that have become a trademark at L&N Seafood. Pastas, chicken, and beef are available for land-lubbers, and these, too, can be ordered the way you like them.

L&N Seafood Grill has a superior reputation for excellent seafood prepared in a good variety of dishes. We all know seafood is a healthy choice at mealtime, and L&N prepares it in such tasty ways that you might forget that it's also good for you! Lexington has a gem in this popular eatery, and the satisfied crowds prove it.

Owner: Morrison, Inc.
         Specialty Restaurant Division
Address: 3199 Nicholasville Road
         Lexington, Kentucky 40503
Telephone: (606) 273-7875
Hours & Days: Sunday-Thursday 11:30 am to 10:00 pm
         Friday-Saturday 11:30 am to 11:00 pm
         Sunday Brunch 11:00 am to 2:00 pm
Reservations not required but taken for preferred seating
American Express, Visa, MasterCard
Directions: Circle 4, exit south at Nicholasville Road;
         downstairs in the Lexington Green Mall.

133

TABLETIZERS
PLENTY TO SHARE WITH FRIENDS.

Fried Zucchini Slices   **2.95**
Fresh zucchini slices with a lightly seasoned coating, sprinkled with parmesan and romano cheeses. Served with a herb cream dip.

Creamy Clam Dip   **3.95**
Fresh sour cream, herbs, spices and clams blended and chilled. Served with wonton chips.

Hot Seafood Cheese Dip   **5.95**
A sharp cheese dip with shrimp, crabmeat and scallops. Served with wonton chips.

Sampler Platter   **6.95**
A sampling of our calamari, zucchini, clam dip and shrimp roll appetizers.

APPETIZERS

New England Clam Chowder   Cup **1.95**
  Bowl **2.95**
Traditional Creamy New England Style.

Creole Gumbo   Cup **2.25**
  Bowl **3.25**
From New Orleans. A hearty soup with Cajun spices, seafood, smoked sausage and vegetables.

Seafood Quesadilla   **3.25**
A southwestern style turnover with shrimp, crabmeat, cheese and spicy seasonings.

Baked Stuffed Mushrooms   **3.50**
Baked mushrooms with a seasoned crabmeat dressing and garlic butter.

Bay Shrimp Cocktail   **2.95**
Four oz. of bay shrimp from the Pacific Northwest. Served with cocktail sauce and lemon.

Shrimp Rolls   **3.50**
Two large Chinese egg rolls stuffed with shrimp, Chinese vegetables and spicy seasonings. Served with an apricot mustard sauce.

Shrimp Cocktail   **5.95**
The traditional favorite.

Fried Calamari   **4.95**
Calamari rings lightly coated in buttermilk and seasoned flour. Served with a zesty marinara sauce.

DINNER SALADS

Blackened Chicken Salad   **6.95**
Strips of spicy blackened chicken breast, salad greens, mushrooms, tomatoes and black olives tossed in a honey mustard dressing.

Oriental Shrimp Salad   **6.95**
Bay shrimp, salad greens, mandarin oranges and garden vegetables tossed in a teriyaki vinaigrette dressing. Served with fried wonton strips.

Spinach Salad with Grilled Salmon   **7.95**
Fresh grilled salmon, spinach, mushroom slices, boiled eggs and croutons tossed in a caper and mustard vinaigrette dressing.

Berry Shrimp Salad   **6.95**
Bay shrimp, salad greens, fresh strawberries, white mushrooms and black olives tossed in a strawberry vinaigrette dressing.

PASTA
SERVED WITH A BOTTOMLESS BOWL OF HOUSE SALAD AND WARM GARLIC CHEESE TOAST.

Linguini with White or Red Clam Sauce   **7.95**
Served in a sauce of tender clams, imported olive oil, garlic, parsley and herbs with your choice of tomato or white sauce.

Baked Seafood Lasagna   **8.95**
Layers of lasagna, ricotta and mozzarella cheeses baked in a marinara sauce, topped with shrimp, crabmeat and scallops in a cheese sauce.

Fettuccine with Shrimp   **11.95**
Fettuccine egg noodles in a cream sauce with whole shrimp, seasonings, herbs, parmesan and romano cheeses.

Shellfish Fettuccine   **12.95**
Shrimp, crabmeat and scallops in a cream sauce, with fresh lemon, garlic, mushrooms and fettuccine egg noodles.

SHRIMP
SERVED WITH A BOTTOMLESS BOWL OF HOUSE SALAD.

Fried Shrimp Small 7.95 Regular 11.95
Hand breaded to order. Served with French fried potatoes, cocktail sauce and lemon.

Shrimp Stir Fry 8.95
Stir fried shrimp and garden vegetables in a teriyaki sauce over rice pilaf. Served with wonton strips.

Grilled Shrimp Skewer Small 8.95 Regular 12.95
Seasoned and grilled over a mesquite charcoal fire. Served over rice pilaf with cocktail sauce and lemon.

Baked Stuffed Shrimp 9.95
Topped with a seasoned crabmeat dressing and a mild cheese sauce. Served with rice pilaf and a vegetable.

Shrimp Scampi 11.95
Shrimp sauteed in butter with garlic, white wine, cream and scallions. Served with rice pilaf and warm garlic cheese toast.

Shrimp Trio 14.95
A sampling of three favorites: mesquite grilled, baked stuffed and fried shrimp. Served with rice pilaf, cocktail sauce and lemon.

COMBINATION PLATTERS
SERVED WITH A BOTTOMLESS BOWL OF HOUSE SALAD.

Shellfish Sampler Platter 11.95
Shrimp, scallops and clam strips, hand breaded to order and fried. Served with tartar and cocktail sauces and French fried potatoes.

Broiled Seafood Platter 14.95
Pan broiled shrimp and scrod, a baked seafood au gratin, rice pilaf and a vegetable.

Fried Fisherman's Platter 13.95
Shrimp, scallops and scrod, hand breaded to order. Served with tartar and cocktail sauces and French fried potatoes.

Cajun Seafood Platter 14.95
A sampling of Cajun favorites. Seared blackened fish, cornmeal fried catfish and shrimp. Served with rice pilaf and a cup of Creole gumbo.

Blackened Ribeye Steak and Broiled Shrimp 15.95
An 8 oz. boneless ribeye seared in a cast iron skillet with Cajun spices and pan broiled shrimp. Served with rice pilaf and a vegetable.

SHELLFISH
SERVED WITH A BOTTOMLESS BOWL OF HOUSE SALAD.

Fried Clams 7.95
Clam strips hand breaded to order and fried. Served with French fried potatoes and tartar sauce.

Maryland Style Crabcakes 10.95
Lightly spiced, broiled crabcake patties. Served with French fried potatoes.

Fried Scallops Small 7.95 Regular 11.95
Fresh scallops, lightly breaded to order and fried. Served with French fried potatoes and tartar sauce.

Rock Lobster Tail Market Price
An 8-oz. cold water lobster tail, lightly seasoned and steamed. Served with a vegetable, buttered red skin potatoes and warm butter.

Alaskan Snow Crablegs (1 1/2 lbs.) Market Price
Steamed Alaskan snow crablegs. Served with a vegetable, buttered red skin potatoes and warm butter.

BEEF AND POULTRY
SERVED WITH A BOTTOMLESS BOWL OF HOUSE SALAD.

Grilled Chicken (10 oz.) 9.95
Breast of chicken, lightly seasoned and grilled over a mesquite charcoal fire. Served with rice pilaf and a vegetable.

Lemon Garlic Chicken (10 oz.) 9.95
Chicken breast, lightly seasoned and grilled with fresh lemon, topped with garlic butter. Served with rice pilaf and a vegetable.

Ribeye Steak (12 oz.) 12.95
A boneless ribeye, mesquite grilled. Served with a baked potato and a vegetable.

Filet Mignon (8 oz.) 14.95
Mesquite grilled. Served with a baked potato and vegetable.

Hot Spiced Shrimp

3 tablespoons kosher salt
1/4 cup pickling spice
2 tablespoons cornstarch

2 quarts cold water
1 pound shrimp,
   medium size, in shells

Combine salt, spice and cornstarch with cold water in a 4-quart sauce-pan. Place pan over medium-high heat and bring to a full boil. Add shrimp to boiling broth and cook exactly 3 minutes from the time broth returns to a boil. Carefully remove shrimp from hot broth and divide into heated bowls. Serve with fresh lemon wedges and your favorite cocktail sauce. Serves 4.

L&N Seafood Grill Drop Biscuits

1 pound L&N Seafood Grill
   biscuit mix

1/4 cup granulated sugar
1 cup ice cold water

Preheat oven to 375 degrees. Measure biscuit mix into a medium-sized bowl and break up any large lumps with spoon. Add sugar to mix; stir to blend ingredients. Add ice cold water to bowl; and, using a large spoon, stir mixture just until water is absorbed into the mix and there is no dry powder. Do not continue to mix batter.

Using a tablespoon or soup spoon, drop batter by spoonfuls onto a lightly-greased cookie sheet and bake for 14 minutes or until biscuits are golden brown. Yields 12 large biscuits.

Shrimp and Crabmeat Omelet

1 tablespoon butter
1/4 cup shrimp, cooked, roughly
   chopped (about 2 ounces)
1/4 cup crabmeat, Snow King,
   lump (about 2 ounces)

11/2 tablespoons green onion,
   thinly sliced
3 whole eggs, beaten well
1 English muffin, toasted

Melt butter in a 7 or 8-inch omelet pan over medium-high heat. Care-fully add the chopped shrimp, crabmeat and green onion; sauté lightly for 1 minute. Pour eggs into pan, stirring to blend all ingredients. Con-tinue to cook over medium heat to allow eggs to begin to set. With a rubber spatula, carefully begin to roll omelet by gently turning the end opposite pan handle over toward center, allowing the unset egg to run onto the pan closest to handle. The omelet will become "cigar" shaped with a moist creamy center. Carefully lift omelet onto center of a warm plate and sprinkle with green onion. Arrange a parsley sprig next to omelet and serve with a toasted English muffin and your favorite brunch accompaniment. Serves 1.

New England Clam Chowder

2 1/4 ounces bacon, finely diced
6 ounces onion, small dice
8 ounces celery, small dice
6 tablespoons flour
2 8-ounce cans clams, chopped
   and drained, reserving juice
2 cups clam juice

1/2 pound potatoes,
   in 1/2 inch cubes
2 teaspoons thyme leaves, whole
1 teaspoon salt
1/2 teaspoon white pepper
1 3/4 cups milk
1 cup heavy cream

Fry bacon in a large, heavy-bottomed soup pot over medium heat until crisp. Stir occasionally to avoid burning. Add onion and celery to pot; cook in bacon fat until onion is transparent. Do not brown.

Stir in flour to make a roux, stirring constantly for 3 to 4 minutes. Slowly add clam juice to the pot, stirring constantly. Add potatoes, reduce heat and simmer until potatoes are tender and broth is thickened. If broth thickens too much, add more clam juice. Add reserved chopped clams and seasoning, stir well and simmer for 5 minutes.

Add milk in 3 stages, simmering 3 minutes between additions. Stir occasionally. Add cream in 2 stages, simmering 1 minute between additions. Stir occasionally. Divide soup into warm cups or bowls. Serves 12 as a first course or 6 as a dinner course.

Citrus Butter

1 large fresh orange, washed
1 large fresh lemon, washed

1 large fresh lime, washed
1 pound butter, softened

Zest the orange, lemon and lime completely (using a zesting tool or a potato peeler). Finely chop the zest and mix together. Cut fruits in half and completely squeeze juice from each, combining the three. Place butter in bowl of an electric mixer and blend on low speed. Add juice slowly and continue to whip until juice is absorbed. Add chopped zest and increase speed, whipping until light and fluffy. Remove from bowl to use as is, or divide it into small portions and freeze to use at a later time.

Delightful as a simple butter sauce on grilled fish, shellfish and chicken. Yields 1 pound.

Vegetable

Rice Pilaf

3 1/4 cups chicken broth, canned
1 bay leaf
1 teaspoon white pepper
3 tablespoons butter

1/2 cup onion, finely diced
1 2/3 cups converted rice
1/2 cup parsley, finely chopped

Preheat oven 425 to 450 degrees. Pour chicken broth into a small sauce-pan; add bay leaf and white pepper. Over medium-high heat, bring to a boil. Melt butter in an oven-proof 2-quart saucepan; add onions and cook until transparent. Add rice to onions; stir until rice becomes very hot and well cooked. Carefully pour boiling broth on rice-onion mixture, stirring well. Bring to a boil. Cover and bake approximately 15 minutes or until liquid is absorbed and rice is tender. Remove pan from oven and gently stir in parsley. Serves 6.

Entrée

Pan Broiled Catch

4 ounces butter, melted
4 fish filets, 6 to 8 ounces each
    (scrod, halibut, snapper, or
    grouper); if fresh, it is not
    necessary to remove skin

Dash salt
Dash white pepper
Dash paprika
2 tablespoons fresh parsley,
    finely chopped

Preheat broiler 425 to 450 degrees. Pour 1/3 of the butter in bottom of a shallow-sided baking dish that is just large enough to easily hold the fish without overcrowding. Arrange filets skin side down in dish and coat each filet with remaining butter. Evenly sprinkle each filet with salt, pepper and paprika.

Place dish under broiler 4 to 6 inches from heat and cook fish for ap-proximately 8 minutes or just until it flakes easily with a fork. Carefully remove dish from broiler and baste fish with some of the cooking butter. Sprinkle fish with parsley. This can be served out of the baking dish or on individual heated plates with boiled parsley potatoes or rice pilaf and a nice vegetable. Serves 4.

Mansion at Griffin Gate

*T*he Mansion at Griffin Gate is a landmark
in Lexington. Located on a grassy hillside just minutes from downtown, this beautiful
antebellum mansion takes you back to a more relaxed and gracious time. Furnished
with antiques, fine paintings, gleaming fireplace mantels, and sparkling crystal and
chandeliers, the Mansion is as beautiful today as it was 130 years ago when built as a
home for a prosperous Lexingtonian.

Today, the Mansion is open for lunch and dinner, and can seat up to 180
people. Each of its nine rooms is named after a variety of tree found on the grounds-
from the Dogwood Room, the large Magnolia Room,to the cool, green Cedar Room.

Chef Dick Lind, having previously worked in several Marriott Hotels, has
prepared a menu befitting the lovely surrounding. The nightly specials allow Chef
Lind to become creative and flexible to the guest's desires.

The Mansion is a wonderful spot to bring a private party of up to 100 for
lunch or dinner. There is a warm feeling that you invited them to your home - if you
lived in a mansion in idyllic surroundings!

The original owners of this lovely home, the Coleman family, would no doubt
be proud of the continued tradition of charm and elegance evoked by the Mansion and
would graciously welcome all the happy guests to "Come again"!

Owner: William B. Terry
     (managed by Marriott Corporation)
Address: 1720 Newtown Pike
     Lexington, Kentucky 40511
Telephone: (606) 231-5152
Hours & Days: Lunch: Monday-Friday 11:30 am to 1:00 pm
         (seasonal)
        Dinner: Monday-Thursday 5:00 pm to 10:00 pm
           Friday-Saturday 5:00 pm to 10:30 pm
           Sunday 5:00 pm to 9:00 pm
Reservations recommended
American Express, Visa, MasterCard, Discover, Carte Blanche, JCB
Directions: 1/2 mile off I-75 at Exit 115, 4 miles from downtown
     Lexington on Newtown Pike; adjacent to Marriott's
     Griffin Gate Resort.

The Mansion
at Griffin Gate

Appetizers

Escargot	6.95
baked in garlic butter	
Shrimp Cocktail	7.95
served with our spicy cocktail sauce	
Scallops with Artichokes	6.95
sauteed in lemon butter	
Smoked Salmon	8.95
garnished with eggs, capers and red onion	
Crepe Royale	8.95
lobster, scallops and shrimp in a rich lobster sauce	

Soups

Baked French Onion   Potage a la Mansion

3.75   3.50

Seafood Bisque

4.75

Salads

Caesar Salad for Two	8.95
prepared tableside	
Spinach Salad	4.50
served with hot bacon dressing	
Mansion Salad	3.50
tossed fresh green salad	

Entrees

Poached Salmon served with strawberry sauce	19.95
Fresh Lemon Sole prepared with lemon butter	19.95
Grilled Swordfish served with herb butter	19.95
Broiled Whole Lobster Maine's finest	Market Price
Tournedos Helder tender filets with lobster tail	26.95
Shrimp a la Mansion in garlic butter	19.95
Steak Au Poivre served with mustard glaze	24.95
Chateaubriand (For Two) tenderloin carved tableside presented with bouquetiere of vegetables	49.00
Rack of Lamb carved tableside with bouquetiere of vegetables	49.00
Steak Diane a favorite prepared tableside with flair	25.95
Veal Oscar topped with crabmeat, asparagus and hollandaise sauce	19.95
Chicken Piccata sauteed chicken breast in lemon butter with capers	17.50

Cajun Shrimp

5 shrimp, 16 to 20 count,
   peeled and deveined
Vegetable oil

1/2 cup spinach leaves, shredded
3 ounces Cajun Sauce*

Sauté shrimp in oil until half done; add sauce and bake at 400 degrees for 8 minutes. Place shrimp over shredded spinach leaves and serve.

Cajun Sauce:
2 ounces onion,
   coarsely chopped
3 ounces celery, chopped
2 ounces green bell pepper,
   coarsely chopped
1 ounce olive oil
1/2 teaspoon white pepper

1/2 teaspoon black peppercorns,
   freshly cracked
1/2 teaspoon red pepper, crushed
1 teaspoon Tabasco
1/2 cup dry white wine
2 cups chicken stock
16 ounces tomato purée

Sauté vegetables in olive oil until tender. Add white, black and red peppers. Cook over high heat for 1 1/2 minutes, stirring constantly. Add Tabasco, white wine, chicken stock, and tomato purée. Simmer 30 minutes. Let cool slightly; blend, and strain. Serves 12.

Cream of Asparagus Soup

4 ounces salad oil
2 medium onions, chopped
2 celery ribs, chopped
2 large carrots, chopped
2 quarts finely-chopped
   asparagus ends
2 quarts chicken stock

3 potatoes, peeled and quartered
2 quarts heavy cream, warmed
1 quart half & half
Salt to taste
Pepper to taste
Nutmeg to taste
Asparagus tips for garnish

Heat oil; add onions, celery and carrots. Cover; sweat vegetables until half cooked, approximately 10 minutes. Add asparagus and chicken stock; bring to a boil. Add potatoes and cook until tender, approximately 20 minutes. Blend until smooth; return mixture to medium heat. Add half & half and seasonings; bring mixture just to a simmer. Add warmed cream, whisking constantly. Garnish with asparagus tips and serve. Serves 20 to 22.

Hot Bacon Dressing for Spinach Salad

l cup white vinegar
1/8 cup brown sugar, packed
3 cups water
1/2 chicken bouillon cube
l tablespoon bacon fat
3 to 4 ounces flour

l tablespoon cracked
   black pepper
l tablespoon garlic, chopped
2 tablespoons Dijon mustard
Salt and pepper to taste
6 pieces cooked bacon

Boil vinegar and sugar for 5 minutes. Add water and bouillon cube. Make roux with bacon fat and flour. Add roux to vinegar mixture and cook 5 minutes longer. Add cracked pepper and garlic. Cool. Add mustard and correct seasonings. Serve with fresh spinach salad. Garnish with bacon pieces.

Hollandaise Sauce

Sauce

3 egg yolks
Juice of 1 lemon
Dash of cayenne pepper

Pinch of salt
1 stick of butter, melted and hot

Place first 4 ingredients in blender. Turn blender on and slowly add butter in a continuous stream. Blend 10 seconds.

Mansion Maître D' Butter

Sauce

1 pound butter, softened
1/3 pound margarine, softened
1/3 cup chopped shallots

1/3 cup warm brandy
8 ounces Dijon mustard
1 1/2 teaspoons
  Worcestershire sauce

Whip butter and margarine together until smooth. Add remaining ingredients. Spread on foil and roll up to 2 inches in diameter. Refrigerate. Cut into 2-ounce portions per steak. Serve under grilled meat. Serves 8.

Poached Salmon with Strawberry Sauce

Entrée

1 6-ounce salmon, butterfly cut
1 ounce Crême de Noyeaux
1 ounce white wine
1 jumbo shrimp,
  peeled and deveined

1 tablespoon strawberry vinegar*
2 ounces heavy cream
1 tablespoon butter
1 parsleyed Puff Pastry Fleuron**
1 strawberry flan***

Place salmon, Crême de Noyeaux and white wine in cold sauté pan. Place shrimp on top of salmon. Heat to simmer on high flame, place shrimp in liquid and cover with buttered parchment. Bake at 350 degrees for 10 minutes or until salmon is cooked through. Remove salmon and shrimp. Return liquid to flame, reduce by 2/3, add strawberry vinegar and cream. Reduce until slightly thickened and finish by whisking in butter. Place sauce on plate, salmon in the middle, shrimp over the salmon and garnish with Fleuron and flan. Serves 1.

*Old strawberries poached twenty minutes in enough red wine vinegar to cover. Strain.

Continued next page

Parsleyed Puff Pastry Fleuron:
Frozen puff pastry

Butter
Parsley, chopped

Cut puff pastry with a wine glass. Cut in half and freeze for several minutes. Bake at 375 degrees for 5 to 7 minutes until brown. The puff pastry will triple in size. Dip in butter, then in chopped parsley.

***Strawberry with cuts to make a fan shape

Entrée

Tournedos Helder

2 4-ounce medallions of
  tenderloin
2 ounces Bordelaise sauce*
1 6-ounce lobster tail, poached
2 ounces Hollandaise sauce**

1/2 teaspoon tarragon
  reduction***
2 tablespoons tomato concassé
  (peeled, deseeded, and chopped)
Chopped parsley

Grill tournedos of beef to desired degree of doneness. Ladle Bordelaise sauce onto round dinner plate and place tournedos on sauce. Remove shell from lobster tail and halve. Place halves on tournedos, forming a circle. Combine Hollandaise and tarragon reduction to make Béarnaise sauce. Ladle Béarnaise over lobster tail halves with tomato concassé and sprinkle with chopped parsley. Serves 1.

*Reduced stock with burgundy
**For recipe, see index

***Tarragon Reduction
1 cup dried tarragon
1/2 cup red wine vinegar

2 shallots, minced
1 tablespoon peppercorns,
  cracked

Combine all ingredients in saucepan. Cook until very little liquid remains.

Dessert

Chocolate Mousse

20 ounces chocolate morsels
6 ounces clarified butter
10 egg yolks

1 cup sugar
3/4 cup Madeira wine
1 1/2 quarts heavy cream,
  sweetened and whipped

Melt chocolate and clarified butter in top of double boiler. Whip egg yolks, sugar and wine in separate mixing bowl over double boiler until mixture thickens, approximately 15 minutes. Add melted chocolate mixture slowly to thickened egg mixture, whisking constantly. Fold in whipped cream; refrigerate 2 hours. Pipe into wine glasses and top with a dollop of whipped cream. Sprinkle with additional chocolate morsels and serve. Serves 20 to 22.

Merrick Inn

The Merrick Inn is so steeped in tradition, that it seems to embody the very soul of Kentucky and its proud history. Built before the Civil War and totally remodeled in 1936, it was the Manor House for one of the finest horse farms in Lexington.

Although many outstanding horses were trained there, one very special thoroughbred, named Merrick, gave Merrick Place its name. His gravestone is located in the front yard at the Inn and proclaims him "worthy in deeds and noble in character".

Bob and Libby Murray own the Merrick Inn today and the graciousness and charm of the Old South lives on in their restaurant. Follow the tree-lined drive from Tates Creek Road to the columned Manor House with manicured grounds. Inside, white clothed tables, fresh flowers, and wood-burning fireplaces offer a relaxed and casual elegance, while in the warmer months, diners can be seated out on the patio by the pool. The Merrick Inn is decorated with period furniture and is a perfect place for parties or simply a quiet evening.

The menu has a decidedly Kentucky flavor. Kentucky Country Ham with Redeye Gravy and Southern Fried Chicken could not be more traditional (nor more delicious), and Stuffed Trout with Cornbread Dressing with crab, shrimp, and onions adds a new twist to a tried and true dish. In addition to the regular menu, there are three or four special entrées nightly, with plenty of fresh seafood, pasta, and even gourmet pizzas.

The Merrick Inn has stayed true to its Kentucky roots, but remains fresh and inviting year in and year out.

Owners: Bob and Libby Murray
Address: 3380 Tates Creek Road
Lexington Kentucky 40502
Telephone: (606) 269-5417
Hours & Days: Monday-Thursday 5:30 pm to 10:00 pm
Friday-Saturday 5:30 pm to 10:30 pm
Bar open 4:30 pm to 1:00 am, except Sundays
Closed all major holidays
Reservations recommended
Visa, MasterCard, American Express, Diner's Club
Directions: Located just inside Circle 4 on Tates Creek
Road, at the top of the hill in Merrick Place
apartment complex.

MERRICK INN

APPETIZERS

Iced Gazpacho with a hint of Cajun $2.75
Snails with Garlic & Fine Herbs $4.95
Grouper Fingers w/Mustard Sauce $3.95
Jumbo Shrimp Cocktail $6.95
Fried Banana Peppers $2.95

Soup of the Day
Cup $1.75

SALADS

Citrus & Avacado with Honey Dressing
Limestone Bibb Lettuce, Tossed Salad
Fruit and Cottage Cheese
Sliced Tomatoes with Homemade
Cucumber Dressing.

PRIME RIB OF BEEF medium rare at its best	14.95
FILET MIGNON No Steak more tender	15.95
CHOICE RIBEYE STEAK Very flavorful, 14 oz	14.50
FILLET OF SOLE a delicious white fish, broiled, lemon butter	10.95
JUMBO OCEAN SHRIMP Deep fried, Plain or with Crab Stuffing	12.95
KENTUCKY COUNTRY HAM The real Thing, Redeye Gravy	11.50
BLUE GRASS LAMB CHOPS 3, 5oz Chops, Mint Jelly	17.95
SOUTHERN FRIED CHICKEN one half, Cut to be eaten with the fingers	10.95
WALL-EYE PIKE my favorite fish, fried	12.95
LOBSTER TAILS South African, 5oz, Broiled, Drawn butter, ONE 16.50, TWO 24.50	
STUFFED TROUT Cornbread Stuffing, w/crab, shrimp, Onions, etc, Broiled	11.50
PROVIMI VEAL LIVER lightly Sauteed, with Onions + Bacon	11.95
LONDON BROIL choice flank Steak, Marinated, Thin Sliced, Au Jus	11.95
ORANGE ROUGHY mild, delicate, whitefish, Broiled Almandine	11.95

All Entrees include, Soup or Salad, Potato, Vegetable, Rolls + butter

VEGETABLES

Baked Potato   Green Beans
Vegetables of the Day

DESSERTS

Dessert of the Day 2.00   Peach Melba 2.75
New York Cheesecake with Strawberries 2.50
Pound Cake with Ice Cream 2.50
Ice Cream & Sherberts

Avocado Crab Cakes with Red Pepper Sauce

l large ripe Hass avocado
Lemon juice
2 tablespoons mayonnaise
l large egg
l tablespoon Dijon mustard
l 1/2 teaspoons green onion,
 chopped

l 18-ounce can crabmeat,
 shells and cartilage removed
3/4 cup unseasoned
 bread crumbs
1/2 cup vegetable oil
Red Pepper Sauce*

Peel and dice avocado, place in a bowl, and sprinkle with lemon juice to prevent discoloring. In a separate bowl, combine mayonnaise, egg, Dijon mustard, and green onion. Add crabmeat and avocado; mix well, then add enough bread crumbs to firm up the mixture. Form into cakes, size dependent upon whether they are eaten as appetizers or entrées. Coat with remaining bread crumbs. Cook in hot vegetable oil until browned, turning once. Serves 4 to 6.

*Red Pepper Sauce:
l cup mayonnaise
1/2 teaspoon dill weed

l teaspoon chopped parsley
l large red pepper,
 roasted, peeled, and puréed

Mix all ingredients together and serve with crab cakes.

Wild Rice Soup with Chicken

3/4 cup butter
l small onion, minced
2 carrots, minced
2 stalks celery, minced
4 garlic cloves, minced
3/4 cup flour
5 cups chicken broth

2 cups cooked wild rice
Dash of sugar
Salt and pepper to taste
3 cups half & half
3 cooked chicken breasts, diced
Chopped parsley for garnish

Melt butter in saucepan; add onion, carrots, celery, and garlic; sauté until tender. Blend in flour, then gradually stir in broth. Cook, stirring constantly, until mixture comes to a boil. Boil and stir for l minute. Add rice, sugar, salt, and pepper. Blend in half & half and diced chicken breasts. Heat to serving temperature and garnish with chopped parsley. Serves 8.

Citrus and Avocado Salad with Honey Dressing

Leaf lettuce
Orange sections
Grapefruit sections

Ripe avocados
Honey Dressing*

Place leaf lettuce on salad plates. With a sharp knife, peel oranges and grapefruits and cut out sections. Arrange sections alternately on lettuce. Top each salad with three or four slices of ripe avocado. Pour Honey Dressing over salads.

Honey Dressing:
Scant 3/4 cup sugar
1 teaspoon paprika
1/8 teaspoon salt
1/3 cup wine vinegar
1 tablespoon onion juice

1 teaspoon celery seed
1 teaspoon dry mustard
1/3 cup honey
1 tablespoon lemon juice
1 cup salad oil

Place all ingredients in a mixing bowl and beat at medium speed for 5 minutes.

Onion Casserole

Vegetable

12 large white onions
Milk for poaching
12 slices of bread, toasted
1 cup American cheese, grated
1 cup medium cheddar cheese, grated

2 eggs
2 cups milk
1 teaspoon salt
1/4 teaspoon paprika
1 1/4 sticks butter

Peel onions and slice crosswise. Poach in milk until tender. Drain well. Place eight slices of toast in a buttered baking dish, arrange onions on top of toast, and sprinkle with American and cheddar cheeses.

Beat well eggs, milk, salt, and paprika. Pour this mixture over onions and cheese and dot with 2 tablespoons butter. Cube remaining 4 slices of toast. Melt remaining butter, and pour over toast cubes, mixing well. Pour over top of casserole and bake at 350 degrees for 40 minutes. Serves 8.

Baked Black Grouper with Orange Butter Sauce

Entrée

3 pounds black grouper, dressed and fileted
1 stick melted butter
1 tablespoon lemon juice

Salt and pepper to taste
Orange Butter Sauce*
Parsley for garnish
Orange slices for garnish

Divide grouper into 8-ounce servings. Mix butter and lemon juice. Dip grouper into mixture, reserving any remaining liquid. Season grouper with salt and pepper. Place in a shallow roasting pan and add a small amount of water to the pan. Bake in hot oven, basting with lemon-butter mixture several times, being careful not to let water completely evaporate. When fish flakes easily with a fork, remove from oven and place on platter. Drizzle Orange Butter Sauce over fish; garnish with orange slices and chopped parsley. Serves 6.

Continued next page

*Orange Butter Sauce
1 6-ounce can frozen orange juice
1/4 cup lemon juice
1/2 teaspoon dry mustard
1/4 teaspoon rosemary

1/2 teaspoon celery salt
1/2 teaspoon onion powder
1/2 teaspoon salt
1 stick butter

Place all ingredients, except butter, in a saucepan and slowly bring to a boil. Boil 1 minute. Remove from heat, cut butter into pieces, add to mixture, and stir until melted. Serve over grouper filets.

Entrée

Long Island Duckling

2 4 1/2- to 5-pound Long Island
  ducks
Soy sauce

Salt and pepper
Rosemary
Chambord Sauce*

Have butcher split two ducks. Wash ducks and trim off excess body and neck fat. Pat ducks dry and rub with soy sauce. Salt and pepper both sides of ducks and place on rack in a shallow roasting pan. Prick each duck several times with a sharp fork to allow fat to escape when roasting. Ducks should be roasted skin side up. Sprinkle with rosemary, and bake at 375 degrees for 1 hour. Remove ducks from pan and pour off excess fat. Return ducks to oven and continue to roast for approximately 45 minutes to 1 hour, or until browned and crisp. Remove from oven and hold in a warm place. Pour Chambord Sauce over ducks. Serves 4.

*Chambord Sauce:
1 10-ounce jar apple jelly

1/2 cup Chambord liqueur
2 tablespoons lemon juice

Place apple jelly in heavy saucepan and melt over low heat, being careful not to burn. Stir to remove lumps. Add Chambord liqueur and lemon juice. Taste, and correct with more lemon juice if mixture is too sweet. Serve over ducks.

Dessert

French Silk Pie

1 1/4 cups graham cracker crumbs
1/4 cup sugar
1/3 cup butter, melted
1 1/4 cups sugar
3/4 cup butter, softened
3 eggs

3 ounces unsweetened chocolate,
  melted and cooled
1 1/2 teaspoons vanilla
1/2 cup whipping cream,
  whipped

In a mixing bowl, combine graham cracker crumbs, sugar and melted butter. Press crumb mixture firmly on bottom and sides of a 9-inch pie plate. Bake at 375 degrees for 8 minutes. Allow to cool.

Cream sugar and butter until light and fluffy. Add eggs, one at a time, beating at medium speed 2 minutes after each addition. Blend in chocolate and vanilla, mixing well. Fold in whipping cream and pour into baked graham cracker crust. Refrigerate at least 2 hours. Serves 6 to 8.

Pampered Chef

Tucked away in the Chevy Chase area of Lexington is an absolute gem of a restaurant called The Pampered Chef. It's the diner, however, that feels pampered in a place where good food and good service are the norm.

The entrance through the long grapevine-trellised walkway serves to set the mood for the cozy interior. Inside, shades of sea foam and salmon are reflected in art work, wall hangings and table cloths. Owner David Larson has created a lovely and intimate setting for Chef John Simpkins outstanding culinary skills. The chef has such a yen to create delicious concoctions that the menu at The Pampered Chef changes every two weeks.

The handsome and affable owner was previously associated with the Watergate Hotel and the Gourmet Gallery Catering firm in Washington, D.C. He opened this popular restaurant in 1982 to rave reviews and happy and consistent crowds of diners.

The Pampered Chef catered over 300 parties in 1988 for groups of up to 400. The restaurant is available for private functions any time not open to the public.

The Pampered Chef appeals to such a diverse clientelle. Everyone seems equally attracted to this spot, and the majority are return customers. Most seem to enjoy the casual, friendly tone and the clublike atmosphere. Add to that the great food, and you have a sure winner.

Owner: David Larson
Address: 314 1/2 South Ashland Avenue
      Lexington, Kentucky 40502
Telephone: (606) 268-1005
Hours & Days: Luncheon: Monday-Friday 11:00 am to 2:00 pm
      Dinner: Friday-Saturday 6:00 pm to 10:00 pm
Available for private functions anytime when not open.
Reservations for dinner only. Luncheon reservations are not accepted.
MasterCard, Visa, American Express
Directions: Located on Ashland Avenue between
      Euclid Avenue and High Street.

THE PAMPERED CHEF

Appetizers....
Cream of Broccoli Soup 1⁹⁵
Bob's Country Ham Paté 3⁹⁵
Fettuccine Alfredo 4²⁵

Salads....
Garden Salad 2⁹⁵
Caesar Salad 3⁵⁰

Entrees....

Filet Leonardo - tenderloin of beef, fresh shrimp and artichoke hearts wrapped and baked in phyllo pastry, served with buerre blanc. 14⁹⁵

Veal Normandy - tender medallions of veal scalloppine, sauteed with granny smith apples, apple brandy and cream 14⁹⁵

Chicken Monterrey - boneless breasts of chicken simmered with scallions, mushrooms, white wine and cream 10⁹⁵

Pan Fried Orange Roughy - fillet of mild New Zealand whitefish rolled in breadcrumbs and meal, panfried, served with Tartare Sauce 12⁹⁵

Sole Florentine - fillet of grey sole rolled around fresh creamed spinach, baked with parmesan sauce 12⁹⁵

Royal Danieli Veal Liver - tender veal liver lightly sauteed with onions, bacon, beef broth and fresh thyme 10⁹⁵

Entrees are served with oven browned potatoes and fresh vegetables

A 15% gratuity is added only to checks for parties of five and more and to all Dining Club checks before any deductions

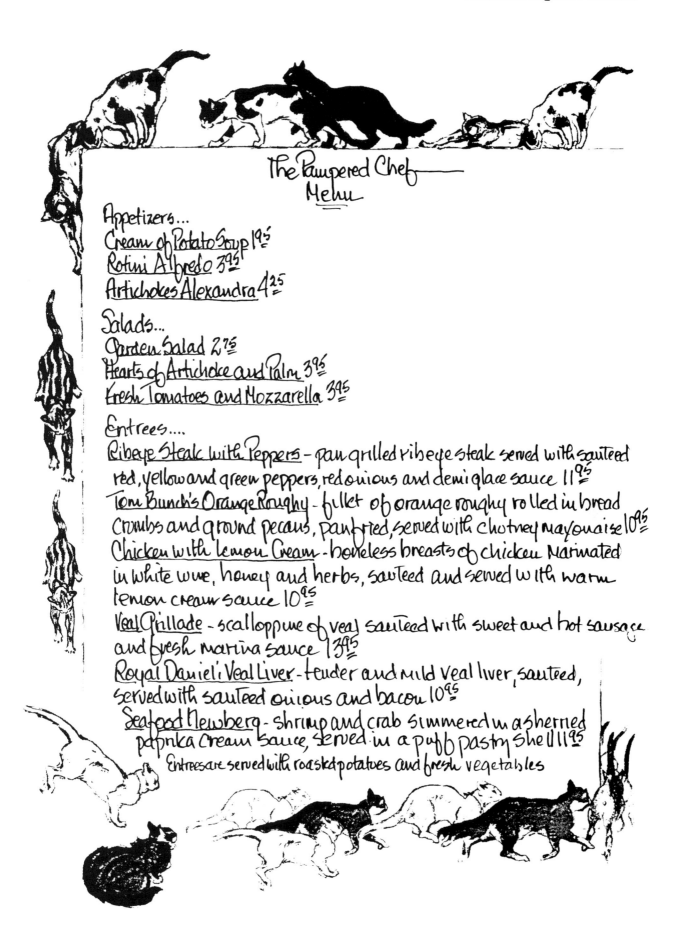

The Pampered Chef
Menu

Appetizers...
Cream of Potato Soup 1⁹⁵
Rotini Alfredo 3⁹⁵
Artichokes Alexandra 4²⁵

Salads...
Garden Salad 2⁷⁵
Hearts of Artichoke and Palm 3⁹⁵
Fresh Tomatoes and Mozzarella 3⁹⁵

Entrees....
Ribeye Steak with Peppers - pan grilled ribeye steak served with sauteed red, yellow and green peppers, red onions and demi glace sauce 11⁹⁵
Tom Bunch's Orange Roughy - fillet of orange roughy rolled in bread crumbs and ground pecans, pan fried, served with chutney mayonaise 10⁹⁵
Chicken with Lemon Cream - boneless breasts of chicken marinated in white wine, honey and herbs, sauteed and served with warm lemon cream sauce 10⁹⁵
Veal Grillade - scalloppine of veal sauteed with sweet and hot sausage and fresh marina sauce 13⁹⁵
Royal Danieli Veal Liver - tender and mild veal liver, sauteed, served with sauteed onions and bacon 10⁹⁵
Seafood Newberg - shrimp and crab simmered in a sherried paprika cream sauce, served in a puff pastry shell 11⁹⁵
Entrees are served with roasted potatoes and fresh vegetables

English Country Pâté

1 tart green apple,
  peeled, cored, chopped
1/4 cup shallots, minced
1 garlic clove
2 tablespoons butter
6 ounces lean boneless pork,
  chopped
6 ounces chicken livers
1 tablespoon brandy

2 tablespoons fresh parsley,
  minced
1 bay leaf, crumbled
Salt and pepper to taste
1/4 cup dry red wine
4 large egg yolks
2 tablespoons heavy cream
1 stick unsalted butter

Cook apples, shallots, and garlic in skillet over moderate heat, stirring for 4 minutes. Add pork and liver; cook until pork is no longer pink. Add brandy, parsley, bay leaf, salt and pepper, and cook 2 minutes longer. Cool 5 minutes.

In food processor fitted with steel blade, purée above mixture with wine. In large bowl, combine yolks and cream; add to purée and combine.

Line a 3-cup terrine with bacon, letting slices hang over sides. Spoon in pâté and smooth top. Fold hanging bacon over pâté. Bake in water bath at 325 degrees for 1 1/2 hours, or until skewer inserted in center comes out clean. Cover terrine with foil and weight with 2-pound weight. Chill overnight.

Remove weight, foil, and bacon from pâté. Wash and dry terrine, and return pâté to terrine. Pour melted butter over pâté and chill, covered, for 2 days. Serves 6.

Vichysquash

2 medium onions, chopped
3 tablespoons butter
12 medium yellow squash,
  thinly sliced

1 cup chicken broth
2 cups light cream
Salt and white pepper to taste
Chopped chives

Sauté onions in butter until transparent. Add squash and chicken broth; simmer 20 minutes. In food processor fitted with steel blade, purée in batches. Add cream to purée, chill thoroughly, and correct seasonings. Serve chilled, garnished with fresh chopped chives. Serves 6.

Seafood Newberg

1/3 cup shallots, chopped
1 stick butter
1 pound shrimp,
  peeled and deveined
1 pound lump crabmeat
1 pound mushrooms, sliced
1/4 cup brandy
1/4 cup cream sherry

4 cups heavy cream
3 tablespoons
  Hungarian paprika
2 tablespoons flour
2 tablespoons butter
Salt and white pepper to taste
12 puff pastry shells

Sauté shallots in butter. Add shrimp and crabmeat; sauté until opaque, about 5 minutes. Add mushrooms and sauté 5 minutes longer. Pour in brandy and sherry and cook 2 minutes. Add cream and paprika, turn heat to low, and simmer 10 minutes. To thicken, use flour and butter. Season with salt and white pepper to taste. Serve in purchased puff pastry shells that have been warmed. Serves 12.

Veal Picata

1 pound veal scallopini,
  thinly sliced
1 cup flour, seasoned with
  salt and white pepper
4 ounces clarified butter

2 tablespoons white wine
1/4 cup lemon juice
1 stick very cold butter,
  cut into pieces
Fresh parsley, chopped

Dredge veal slices in seasoned flour, shaking off excess. Melt clarified butter in skillet over moderate heat. Sauté veal and place on warm platter as finished. Veal cooks quickly, so sauté only 2 minutes per side. After sautéing veal, add wine and lemon juice to skillet and reduce by half. Quickly whisk in cold butter, remove skillet from heat, and continue whisking until butter is incorporated. Return veal to skillet to coat with sauce. Place veal on warm platter, pouring any remaining sauce over it. Garnish with chopped parsley. Serves 4.

Dessert

Daiquiri Soufflé

10 large eggs, separated
2 cups sugar
Grated rind of 2 lemons
Grated rind of 2 limes
1/2 cup lemon juice

1/2 cup lime juice
1/2 cup rum
2 packages unflavored gelatin
3 cups whipping cream
Lime slices, paper thin

With mixer, beat yolks and 1 cup sugar until thick and tripled in bulk. Add rinds and juices. Cook mixture, stirring constantly, over very low heat until mixture coats the back of a spoon. Soften gelatin in rum, and stir into warm mixture.

With mixer, beat egg whites until stiff peaks form, adding 1 cup sugar gradually. Gently fold egg whites into egg mixture. Beat whipping cream until just fluffy and fold into mixture. Pour into glass bowl or wine glasses and refrigerate until set, about 6 hours. Garnish with whipped cream and paper thin lime slices. Serves 14.

Dessert

Viennese Apple Tart

1/2 cup sugar
2 1/2 cups flour
Grated rind of 1 lemon
1/2 pound unsalted butter, cold,
   cut into small pieces
2 egg yolks
6 cups sliced Delicious apples
2/3 cup sugar

2 tablespoons cornstarch
1/4 teaspoon nutmeg
1 teaspoon cinnamon
1/4 cup golden raisins
1/2 cup chopped pecans
1/4 cup apricot preserves
1/2 stick unsalted butter

In food processor fitted with steel blade, process sugar, flour, rind, and butter until consistency of meal. Add yolks and process until bound together. Press dough onto bottom and sides of a 9 or 10-inch tart pan with detachable bottom. A springform pan may be used. Bake at 400 degrees for 10 minutes. Let cool.

Mix peeled apples, sugar, cornstarch, nutmeg, cinnamon, raisins, and nuts until dry ingredients coat apples. Set aside.

Melt preserves and coat bottom of partially done crust. Add apples and dot with butter. Bake at 400 degrees for 10 minutes, then reduce heat to 375 degrees and cook for 35 to 40 minutes more. Serves 6 to 8.

Pegasus

The Pegasus Restaurant is located in the beautiful and immensely popular Marriott at Griffin Gate. Here, 250 lush and tranquil acres surround a resort that blends the gracious traditions of the Old South with the comfort and convenience of today.

The Pegasus ranks with the finest hotel restaurants in Kentucky, and has an ambiance that is classy without being stuffy, and food that is sophisticated yet straightforward.

Stepping up into the Pegasus, the diner retreats to a room that exudes comfort and seclusion. Polished oak and gleaming brass are set against burgandy and dark green. Fresh flowers, green leafy plants, and friendly service invite a leisurely dinner.

The Pegasus specializes in beef and seafood, and the chef creates a different veal dish each night called Veal Pegasus. Two fresh vegetables accompany most entrées, unless you order Stir-fry Shellfish, which is chocked full of shrimp, scallops, lobster and veggies in a soy-ginger sauce. Mmmm!

Desserts are listed on a separate menu and range from Chocolate Macadamia Nut Pie to Cheesecake or traditional Southern Pecan Pie.

The combination of low-key atmosphere and first-rate dining has gained the Pegasus a well-deserved place in the limelight.

Owners: Marriott's Griffin Gate Resort
Address: 1800 Newton Pike
          Lexington, Kentucky 40511
Telephone: (606) 231-5100
Hours & Days: Sunday-Thursday 6:00 pm to 10:00 pm
                 Friday-Saturday 6:00 pm to 10:30 pm
Reservations recommended
Visa, MasterCard, American Express, Diner's Club, Carte Blanche, Discover
Directions: Located off the main lobby of Marriott's Griffin Gate Resort.
          Newton Pike and I-75.

Appetizers

Fresh Shrimp Cocktail
served with cocktail sauce
6.95

Escargot With Brie Cheese
sauteed in garlic butter
6.50

Seafood Platter
jumbo shrimp, crabclaws
and smoked salmon
7.95

Baked Oysters J.W.!
plump oysters topped with
crab meat, cheese sauce and
parmesan cheese.
6.75

Baked French Onion Soup
au gratin
3.50

Soup Du Jour
made fresh daily
2.25

Salads

Pegasus Salad
romaine lettuce with bay
shrimp and parmesan cheese
tossed tableside
3.50

Garden Salad
choice of dressing
2.50

Spinach Salad
served with hot bacon dressing
3.50

Entrees

Live Maine **LOBSTER** *market price*

Filet Mignon
*broiled filet mignon
topped with Marriott steak sauce*
18.95

Prime Rib of Beef
*slow oven roasted
served with au jus*
16.95

Filet and Lobster Tail
classic surf and turf
Market Price

Poached Salmon
*pink alaskan filet served
with our dill hollandaise sauce*
17.50

Veal Pegasus
chef's own creation
18.50

Cajun Grouper
*fresh filet of grouper
with Cajun spicing*
16.95

New York Strip
*open flame broiled
topped with Marriott steak sauce*
16.95

Swordfish
fresh grilled swordfish
17.95

Stirfry Shellfish
*stirfry with shrimp,
scallops, lobster,
in a soy ginger sauce
served with fried rice*
19.95

Pasta Fruit De Mer
*slightly sauteed shrimp,
scallops and lobster, tossed
with pasta and sherry cream
served with a touch of parmesan*
18.95

DESSERT MENU AVAILABLE

Escargot

6 boiled red "B" potatoes   6 escargot
4 tablespoons garlic butter   6 small pieces brie cheese

Cut ends of potatoes and hollow out one end with a melon baller. Fill with garlic butter, then escargot. Bake at 350 degrees until hot. Remove and place 1 piece of brie over each escargot. Return to oven and heat until cheese begins to melt. Serves 1.

Oysters J. W.

2 tablespoons Béchamel Sauce*   1 teaspoon Parmesan cheese,
4 oysters on half shell   grated
2 tablespoons crabmeat   2 tablespoons
                                      Hollandaise Sauce**

Spoon Béchamel Sauce over oysters. Cover with crabmeat and sprinkle with Parmesan cheese. Place filled oysters in shells into pan and heat in oven to brown cheese. Remove and top with Hollandaise Sauce. Serves 1.

*Béchamel Sauce: 1 small onion studded with 2 or
2 tablespoons butter   3 whole cloves
2 tablespoons flour   1/2 small bay leaf
1 cup milk   Salt and pepper to taste
                                   Dash nutmeg

Make a roux with butter, flour and milk. Add onion and bay leaf; stir until smooth. Bake at 350 degrees for 20 minutes. Remove and strain. Season to taste.

**see index for recipe

Pegasus Salad

4 ounces Romaine lettuce,   1/4 cup Parmesan cheese, grated
   chopped   2 ounces bay shrimp, cooked
2 ounces Dijon Vinaigrette*
   Dressing

Toss all ingredients together and serve on a chilled plate. Serves 1.

*see index for recipe

Seafood Salad Platter

1 cup leaf lettuce,
  finely shredded
3 shrimp, cooked,
  peeled and deveined
3 crab claws, cooked
4 pieces Scottish
  smoked salmon, rolled
1 teaspoon capers

1 teaspoon hard-boiled egg,
  chopped
1 teaspoon red onion, diced
1 cucumber cup
1 1/2 ounces purchased
  cocktail sauce
1 lemon wrap

Spread lettuce over half of the plate. Alternate shrimp and crab claws over lettuce. Place salmon on empty quarter of plate. Sprinkle with capers, egg, and red onion. Place cucumber cup filled with cocktail sauce and lemon wrap stuck with cocktail fork on remaining quarter of plate. Serves 1.

Blackened Grouper

1 8 ounce grouper filet

2 ounces Cajun seasoning

Coat grouper with seasoning and blacken each side in HOT cast iron skillet until done. Serves 1.

Seafood Fettuccine with Sherry Cream Sauce

3 large shrimp
3 pieces lobster tail (1/2 tail)
6 sea scallops
1 1/2 ounces butter, clarified
3 fresh mushrooms, sliced
5 fresh snow peas
2 ounces sherry
6 ounces heavy cream

6 ounces fettuccine,
  cooked and drained
4 ounces Parmesan cheese,
  grated
1 1/2 tablespoons parsley,
  chopped
1 egg

Sauté shrimp, lobster and scallops in butter 1/2 minute. Add mushrooms and snow peas; sauté an additional 1/2 minute. Deglaze with sherry and reduce by half. Add cream, fettuccine, cheese, and parsley; reduce 1 to 2 minutes. Remove from heat and stir in egg, mixing well. Serves 1.

Dessert

Hot Apples with Cinnamon Ice Cream

1 dollop whipped cream,
  sweetened
1 ice cream cone cup

5 ounces hot apple filling
1 scoop cinnamon ice cream

Place dollop of whipped cream on plate and cone cup on top (to keep cone from sliding). Fill cone with hot apple filling and scoop cinnamon ice cream on top. Serves 1.

Dessert

Little Devil

1 brownie
1 scoop ice cream
2 ounces hot fudge

1 dollop whipped cream,
  sweetened

Place brownie on serving dish and scoop ice cream on top. Cover with hot fudge; top with whipped cream. Serves 1.

1880 Restaurant & Bar

Located in an 1880 Italiante mansion in the historic South Hill section of Lexington, 1880 is a new restaurant named for its historic past. Although they have only been open since last spring, this is already such a popular restaurant that it always seems to have been there. Perhaps that's because the owner, Mesut Sakar, knows a little something about the restaurant business. He served as maître d' at the Coach House for 8 years and also worked at the 21 Club and the Russian Tea Room in New York.

Mesut took this architectural treasure and artfully decorated it so as to make the most of the grace and charm of the high ceilings, winding staircase, and shimmering crystal chandeliers. What transpired were elegantly marbelized walls, tapestry covered chairs, architectural drawings and a romantic spray of roses on each table.

The rich and varied menu features internationally classic gourmet cuisine and is an equal match for the lovely surroundings. There are twenty intriguing entrées and Chef Edward Brinegar loves to offer specials from around the world. The wine menu is second to none in international variety. Even the coffee is unique - chosen carefully and ground on the premises.

The menu of 1880 changes twice yearly so as to better compliment the season. Mesut Sakar promises that "There is something here for everyone's taste...each an unforgettable dining experience".

Owner: Mesut Sakar
Address: 270 South Limestone
   Lexington, Kentucky 40508
Telephone: (606) 253-1880
Hours & Days: Lunch: Monday-Friday 11:30 am to 2:30 pm
     Dinner: Monday-Thursday 5:30 pm to 10:00 pm
      Friday-Saturday 5:30 pm to 11:00 pm
Reservations recommended
MasterCard, Visa, American Express, Diner's Club
Directions: Downtown Lexington, on South Limestone between
   Maxwell and Vine Streets.

1880
RESTAURANT & BAR

Appetizers

CARPACCIO	$7.50		**TORTELLINI PROVENCAL**	$4.50
Shaved, marinated New York Strip.			*Cheese filled pasta sauteed with tomatoes, garlic and white wine.*	
PATE DE MAISON	$4.50		**FETTUCCINI ALFREDO**	$4.50
IRISH SMOKED SALMON	$8.00		*Egg noodles in a classic cream sauce.*	
Caper, onion, cream cheese garni.				
GRILLED SHRIMP	$7.50		**BAKED SCALLOPS**	$6.00
Served with orange saffron cream sauce.			*on artichoke bottoms with sauce Choron.*	
BRIE EN CROUTE	$6.00		**ESCARGOT BOURGUIGNONNE**	$6.50
with fresh fruit garni.			**EGGPLANT ROULADE**	$6.00
OYSTERS 1880	$7.50		*Filled with cream cheese and crabmeat served on black bean mayonnaise.*	
Baked on the half shell with fresh spinach, country ham and Brie.				

Soups

Du Jour *$2.50*   Kentucky Burgoo *$3.00*   French Onion *$3.00*   Potage St. Germain *$3.00*

Salads

NICOISE	$5.00		**SEAFOOD CHEF**	$5.00
Marinated new potatoes, snap peas and grilled tuna over a bed of mixed greens. Served chilled.			*Sauteed shrimp and scallops in a sherry cream sauce served warm over Bibb leaves with bell peppers and water chestnuts.*	
SPINACH	$4.00		**CAESAR**	$4.00
Fresh leaves of spinach, boiled egg, sliced peppers and mushrooms, served with hot bacon dressing.			*The Classic, prepared for one.*	

A La Carte

Sugar Snap Peas	$2.50	*French Fried Sweet Potatoes*	$2.00
Tempura Mushrooms	$3.00	*Steamed Broccoli with pecan butter*	$3.00
Bluecheese sauce		*Baked Potato*	$2.00
Hearts of palm mornay	$3.50		

Dessert

French Vanilla Yogurt	$2.50	*Cheesecake with fresh fruit*	$3.50
Raspberry or Lemon Sorbet	$2.50	*or chocolate sauce*	
Rice Pudding	$2.50	*Fresh Fruit Crepes*	$5.00
Double Chocolate Ice Cream	$2.50	*Dessert Cart*	$3.75

Entrees

Served with house salad, potato and vegetable du jour.

AUSTRALIAN ROCK LOBSTER	$32.50
Broiled jumbo cold water lobster tail, served with drawn butter.	
STEAK PROVENCE	$22.00
Filet mignon, lump crab meat filled char grilled served with a roquefort cheese demi glace sauce.	
STEAK AU POIVRE	$20.00
With demi glace Cabernet Sauvignon sauce.	
FILET MIGNON	$20.00
Char-grilled with either Bearnaise or Diane sauce.	
LAMB CHOPS	$20.00
Grilled with fresh herbs, served with English mint sauce.	
STEAK A LA RUSSE	$19.00
With sour cream and demi glace sauce.	
SIS KEBAB	$18.50
Marinated leg of lamb grilled en-brochette served with a rice-orzo pilaf.	
FETTUCCINI MARINARA	$18.50
Sauteed shrimp, scallops, and salmon with spinach and egg fettucine sprinkled with mozzarella cheese.	
HALIBUT DIJONNAISE	$18.50
Baked with a glaze of pommery and dijon mustard sauce.	
VEAL CHOP	$18.00
Grilled with basil butter.	
WEINER SCHNITZEL	$18.00
Lightly breaded veal sauteed with fresh lemon, anchovies and caper garni.	
SWORDFISH NICOISE	$18.00
Grilled with a sauce of tomatoes, olives, garlic and white wine.	
SALMON FILLET	$18.00
Broiled, served with fresh dill sauce	
NEW YORK STRIP	$18.00
Char-grilled.	
SCALLOPS ETOUFFEE	$17.00
Blackened scallops served with etouffee sauce.	
CHICKEN MAISON	$16.00
Breast of chicken rolled with smoked salmon, served on a bed of sauteed fresh spinach with sauce Bearnaise.	
PISTACHIO CHICKEN	$15.00
Baked chicken breast filled with Swiss cheese and pistachio nuts, served in frangelico cream sauce	
TEMPURA SHRIMP	$15.00
Lightly battered, served with a sherry plum sauce.	
CHICKEN KIEV	$14.00
Lightly breaded chicken breast filled with herb butter and baked.	
CHICKEN PICCATA	$13.00
Lightly breaded breast of chicken, sauteed and served with browned lemon butter.	
PASTA PRIMAVERA	$12.00
Fettuccini noodles with sauteed fresh vegetables, sun-dried tomatoes and crumbled feta cheese.	

Baked Scallops

Sauce Choron*
12 ounces sea scallops
1 ounce white wine
4 ounces water
8 artichoke bottoms
2 carrots,
   julienned matchstick size
1 zucchini, julienned

1 yellow squash, julienned
Salt and pepper
Lemon juice
1/4 head purple cabbage,
   shredded
4 lemon wedges
4 sprigs fresh herbs

Prepare Sauce Choron not more than 2 hours ahead. Poach scallops in sauté pan with wine and water. When almost done, add artichoke bottoms and heat thoroughly. Sauté carrots 1 minute. Add zucchini and yellow squash and sauté. Cover individual plates with juliennes. Place 2 artichoke bottoms and 3 scallops on each. Top with small amount of Choron Sauce. Garnish with shredded purple cabbage, lemon wedge, and herb sprigs. Serves 4.

*Sauce Choron:
4 egg yolks
Juice of 2 lemons
Dash of white wine
1/4 teaspoon salt

4 ounces clarified butter
Dash white pepper
Dash cayenne pepper
Dash Worcestershire sauce
2 tablespoons ketchup

Place egg yolks, lemon juice, wine and salt in top of double boiler. Whisk constantly until eggs double in volume and hold thick ribbons. Remove from heat and whisk 2 minutes more. Add butter in a thin stream. Add remaining seasonings and ketchup. Transfer to bowl and cover with plastic wrap until ready to use. (Classic Choron has a tarragon reduction, but a milder version is desired with this dish.)

Tortellini Provençal

2 cups frozen cheese tortellini
2 ounces clarified butter
1 cup tomatoes concassé (peeled,
   seeded, and chopped)
2 ounces dry white wine

2 ounces water
1/2 tablespoon fresh garlic,
   chopped
Juice of 1/2 lemon
Salt and white pepper to taste

Thaw pasta according to package instructions. Heat butter in sauté pan; add pasta and heat, shaking constantly. Add tomatoes and heat thoroughly. Increase heat, add wine, and boil 30 seconds. Add water and reduce heat. Add garlic, lemon juice, salt, and pepper. Simmer until sauce coats spoon well. Serves 4.

Chef's Seafood Salad

1 ounce clarified butter
1/4 green bell pepper
1/4 red bell pepper
6 water chestnuts, sliced
4 large shrimp, peeled and
  deveined
5 to 6 ounces sea scallops
2 ounces dry sherry

6 ounces heavy cream
Juice of 1/4 lemon
1 tablespoon Romano cheese,
  grated
1 large or 2 small heads hydro
  Bibb lettuce
Lemon twists for garnish

Melt butter in sauté pan; add peppers and chestnuts. Cook 1 minute over moderate heat. Add shrimp and scallops; cook 1 minute more. Deglaze with sherry. Turn heat to high to flame off alcohol. Stir in cream and reduce heat. Add lemon juice and cheese; simmer to desired consistency.

Quarter heads of lettuce from top, fold open on plate and spoon sauce and ingredients over top. Garnish with lemon twists. Serves 2.

Chicken Maison

4 8-ounce chicken breasts,
  skinned and boned
8 ounces smoked salmon,
  thinly sliced
1 ounce butter
3 ounces water
Salt and pepper to taste

6 ounces fresh spinach
1 medium shallot, minced
Butter for sautéing
Dash Pernod
Water
Béarnaise Sauce*

Lightly pound chicken breast and remove excess fat. Lay 2 ounces of smoked salmon on inside of chicken and roll side to side so connective breastbone runs the length of chicken. Repeat with remaining chicken and 2-ounce portions of salmon. Brush pan and chicken with butter. Add water, salt, and pepper; bake at 350 degrees in convection oven for approximately 12 minutes.

Sauté spinach and minced shallots in a small amount of butter. Season with salt and pepper. Add Pernod and a splash of water and heat. Slice chicken on bias and lay, ends turned outwards, on a bed of spinach. Top with Béarnaise Sauce. Serves 4.

Béarnaise Sauce
Prepare Choron Sauce (see recipe above), omitting ketchup and adding following:

3 tablespoons dried tarragon
1 tablespoon crushed black
  peppercorns

1 small shallot, minced
1/4 cup wine vinegar
1/4 cup white wine

Combine all ingredients with Choron Sauce and simmer until only 2 tablespoons liquid remain. Blend with Hollandaise (see index for recipe).

Entrée

Kentucky Bourbon Steak

Marinade:
5 cloves garlic
3/4 cup bourbon whiskey
1/2 cup olive oil

1/2 cup soy sauce
1 inch piece ginger root, minced

1 pound flank steak, cleaned and scored

Sauce:
2 ounces clarified butter
1 cup mushrooms
1/4 cup flour
1 1/2 to 2 cups beef stock

Dash Worcestershire sauce
Salt and pepper to taste
1 ounce or more bourbon, to taste
1 medium onion, optional

Process marinade ingredients in food processor. Blend thoroughly. Marinate flank steak for 1 to 3 days.

For sauce: Sauté mushrooms in butter 2 minutes. Stir in flour to make a paste. Add 1/2 cup beef stock, blend thoroughly, and add remaining stock and ingredients. Boil 5 minutes, stirring constantly. Reduce heat and simmer to desired consistency.

Grill flank steak and slice on thin bias. Serve over sautéed onions. Serves 4.

Entrée

Steak Provence

1 7-ounce filet of beef,
  chateau cut
2 ounces lump crabmeat
1/4 ounce butter or margarine
Butter for brushing meat

Salt and pepper to taste
Sauce Provence*
1 tablespoon Roquefort
  cheese crumbles

Prepare sauce ahead. Cut slit in side of filet, working knife in and around to form a pocket. Stuff with crabmeat and pat of butter. Close opening with toothpick, if necessary. Grill to desired doneness and serve bedded on sauce with a thin ribbon of sauce over the top. Sprinkle with crumbled cheese on and around filet. Serves 1.

Sauce Provence:
2 cups beef stock
1/2 cup red wine
1/4 teaspoon thyme

3 cloves garlic, minced
1/4 cup cornstarch and
  water paste
1/4 cup Roquefort cheese

Bring to a boil stock, wine, thyme and garlic; reduce by 1/4. While boiling, add enough cornstarch paste to achieve coating consistency. Add cheese and remove from heat. Serves 15.

INDEX

LEXINGTON IN GOOD TASTE

Mail to:
McClanahan Publishing House, Inc.
P.O. Box 100
Kuttawa, Kentucky 42055

**For orders CALL TOLL FREE
1-800-544-6959
Visa & MasterCard accepted**

Please send me_____copies of

LEXINGTON IN GOOD TASTE @ $10.95 each_____
Postage and Handling @ $2.00 each_____
Kentucky residents add 5% sales tax @ .55 each_____
Total _____

Make check payable to McClanahan Publishing House

Ship to:
Name_____

Address_____

City_____State_____Zip_____

LEXINGTON IN GOOD TASTE

Mail to:
McClanahan Publishing House, Inc.
P.O. Box 100
Kuttawa, Kentucky 42055

**For orders CALL TOLL FREE
1-800-544-6959
Visa & MasterCard accepted**

Please send me_____copies of

LEXINGTON IN GOOD TASTE @ $10.95 each_____
Postage and Handling @ $2.00 each_____
Kentucky residents add 5% sales tax @ .55 each_____
Total _____

Make check payable to McClanahan Publishing House

Ship to:
Name_____

Address_____

City_____State_____Zip_____